Kansas City, Missouri
An Architectural History
1826-1976

HISTORIC
KANSAS CITY
FOUNDATION

Published by Historic Kansas City Foundation / Kansas City, Missouri

Kansas City, Missouri
An Architectural History
1826-1976

George Ehrlich

The publication of this book has been made possible by
grants received from the following:

The Hallmark Educational Foundation
Carrie J. Loose Trust
Lucile M. Pritchard Trust
Enid and Crosby Kemper Foundation
Parmelee Foundation, Inc.
J. B. Reynolds Foundation
Kuehn Foundation

FIRST EDITION

Copyright 1979 by George Ehrlich

L.C. 79-64507   ISBN 0-913504-52-1

Printed in the United States of America
The Lowell Press, Kansas City, Missouri

The publication of this book benefits
Historic Kansas City Foundation

Detail from Fig. 194

Table of Contents

Detail from Fig. 177

Preface

Why a History of Kansas City Architecture?

First, there are the buildings themselves. Buildings do beckon us. But the buildings are more than works of art and engineering, they are also incomparable documents in the history of the city.

Kansas City and its architectural history had their origins in the first shelters provided for a permanent settlement. This was a frontier trading post launched in the decade of the 1820s. Subsequent growth, into the city we know today, is reflected in the architecture that succeeding generations built. What we see, and knowledge of what no longer stands, tell us that the changes over the years have been considerable.

When compared to such long-lived cities as Rome or London, Kansas City's span of slightly more than 150 years does not seem very significant. Even when compared to the older urban centers of the United States, such as Boston or Philadelphia, Kansas City seems too young and too small to deserve the special attention of the architectural historian. Yet we know that the age and size of a city need not limit its importance for the urban historian. And whatever its location, size or age, a city presents the historian with a complex of buildings that can tell the willing viewer a great deal.

The study of individual buildings and their groupings, shows us that architecture is not only a record of a city's development, but that it is, in fact, an active participant in the dynamics of a city's growth. But no study of architecture should forget that buildings can be works of art. They and their designers and builders deserve attention for this reason too. The fact that we can and do "read" and react to buildings with this duality of orientation makes the study of architecture both challenging and difficult. It also accounts for some of the hesitancy historians have in preparing architectural histories of an entire city.

In the case of Kansas City and its architecture, one will discover that until fairly recently very little has been published. In this respect, Kansas City is no different than a great many other American cities. However, if we are to comprehend the unique characteristics of an American city, we must know its architectural history. Further, we can never assume that past neglect is indicative of the quality of the architectural record, and it can never be an excuse to continue to neglect a city's architectural history. Neglect of this sort inevitably will be reflected in neglect of the physical architecture itself. This has occurred in Kansas City to its detriment, as is all too clearly evident. It has also occurred in other cities as well.

The lack of a substantial bibliography of earlier studies of the architecture of Kansas City has complicated the preparation of a general survey. We may, in fact, have been too bold to attempt one before there were more specialized studies on which to draw. But we needed to begin somewhere, and a general survey (whatever its inadequacies) may stimulate others to do and publish the necessary specialized research that in time will be the basis for a comprehensive history of the physical fabric of the city. It may also make the general reader more sensitive to the city and its architecture. This then has been our motivation.

The Approach

Written sources, fewer than desirable, have been important. These have ranged from some books and a few magazine articles, through newspaper accounts, to city records. But more important, there have been the visual sources. These have been the buildings and urban views that have been studied first hand for a good many years, since the autumn of 1954 when the writer first came to live in Kansas City. A great many have been photographed in the process, some before substantial modification or demolition erased their contributions to the cityscape. In addition, there are those buildings and views that are now known only through old photographs, an occasional drawing or print, and published illustrations. Finally, there are maps of all sorts, ranging from pictorial, bird's-eye delineations to Geologic Survey quadrangles, that provide invaluable insight into the past appearance of a city.

Yet with all these sources, available to me and to others, less than ten years ago we knew very little about Kansas City's architecture. Even the city's general history has received less study than it deserved. The fact that I can now bring together enough data to support this survey is an indication that recently a great many people have been and are at work on the general subject of Kansas City's architectural history. I have drawn on their work, most of which is not yet published. Many of these people have been or are associated with the Landmarks Commission, the Historic Kansas City Foundation, and the Kansas City Chapter of the American Institute of Architects.

Concurrent with my reading, looking and photographing, data on individual buildings and architects were assembled. Much of this came from newspapers and the City Directories, but an even larger amount came from the work of other investigators as noted above. As my knowledge grew, about the city's history on the one hand and about the architecture on the other, correlations between the two suggested themselves. These led me to a number of attempts to group this conglomerate of visual and verbal data into several develop-mental periods. Some lectures and papers drawn from these efforts solidified basic concepts and tested them.

When it came to the actual writing, I held firm to the policy that I would select buildings rather than architects to illustrate the architectural development of the city. As a consequence, some fine architects are either not mentioned or inadequately represented, while at times another architect or firm might appear repeatedly and be represented by several examples. There are two reasons for taking an approach that neglects people. First, there was a need to avoid the dilemma of how to give a fair cross-sectional representation to a rather large cast of characters, when the number of examples one will use will be necessarily limited. Second, while people—architects, clients, developers, and preservationists—are very important in the history of a city's architecture, my intent was to concentrate on the *problems* they faced, the *influences* upon them, and the *results* of their efforts, as these occurred over the years.

This then is a history of a city as it can be read in the architecture that was built. It is a study of buildings that stand or once stood in Kansas City, Missouri. The history of the architects who designed these buildings must wait on another day.

The Illustrations

With few exceptions, all of the illustrations, whether original photographs or photocopies, were taken by me using a Mamiya C220, 2¼ twin-lens, reflex camera. The lens most frequently used was a 55mm Sekor. In addition, 85mm and 250mm Sekor lenses were used. In almost every instance, a medium-yellow filter has been used for original exterior views. The few exceptions noted above are the photographs taken before 1971, when a twin-lens Rolleicord was used. In the majority of cases, photographs were taken on Kodak Verichrome film, developed in D-76, and the negatives were printed on 8 x 10 Kodak Polycontrast paper (F surface) and developed in Dektol.

In general, it has been my practice to photograph buildings from the normal vantage points of a pedestrian (assuming binoculars might substitute for a long focal length lens). A

x

tripod was used when convenient, but this was not feasible for many of the photographs. Long experience has dictated that one must take advantage of circumstance in photographing architecture, and thus it was not always possible to have a tripod along with the other photographic gear. Postponing a photograph until better lighting, or less congested traffic conditions, or having the luxury of a tripod, might mean no photograph at all. Thus, one must acknowledge an unevenness in the quality that can be found in the photographs. At some point one simply has to say that there wasn't time to do it better. One can hope to return another day and do it better.

Photocopies were made under a variety of ad hoc conditions, using the ambient light available in the libraries. Here too, the concern was to "get the picture" when the opportunity was present, rather than delay until ideal copy conditions could be set up.

All given addresses for the illustrated buildings are within the corporate limits of Kansas City, Missouri (as of 1978) unless otherwise indicated. Dates for buildings are drawn from various sources and represent the best information available to the writer at the time of publication. Materials photocopied are identified by the collection of which they are a part. Frequently cited collections are identified by abbreviations as follows:

MC, MVR-KCPL	Montgomery Collection, Missouri Valley Room, Kansas City, Missouri Public Library.
MVR-KCPL	General Collections, Missouri Valley Room, Kansas City, Missouri Public Library.
NSC, MVR-KCPL	Native Sons Collection, Missouri Valley Room, Kansas City, Missouri Public Library.
SC-UMKC	Special Collections, General Library, University of Missouri-Kansas City.

Acknowledgments

It is difficult to recognize everyone's contribution to my learning, but especially important to my efforts have been the assistance of the staff of the Missouri Valley Room of the Kansas City, Missouri Public Library, particularly Peggy Smith and David Boutros. I am also indebted to the ongoing research of the staff of the Landmarks Commission, which they have always generously shared.

I have been aided by two research grants, for the photo-documentation of historically significant architecture in the Kansas City metropolitan area, which were received from the Research Administration of the University of Missouri-Kansas City.

The Historic Kansas City Foundation has proved to be most supportive in the long period during which all of this went forward. Jody Craig, Executive Director of HKCF, and Ellen Goheen of the HKCF Board of Directors, did much to make a publication out of a manuscript and a stack of photographs. Beth Ellington performed the difficult and important task of editor. Ellen Uguccioni prepared the index.

And then there has been the good humor and encouragement of my wife, Mila Jean Ehrlich, who has put up with some rather eccentric behavior for a good many years, and has shared my fascination with the problems and the buildings. Her continued support has been critical. Finally, had it not been for Suzanne Statland, of the HKCF Board of Directors and formerly of the Landmarks Commission, who linked me with the Kansas City Landmarks Commission from 1973 to 1975, and provided early encouragement, I might never have dared to look for a rational pattern in what once seemed to be nothing but fragments of murky data. If I have succeeded in bringing some order to all of this material, and if my interpretations are reasonably correct, it is only because so many other people have been so unselfish in their assistance.

GEORGE EHRLICH
Kansas City, Missouri
January, 1979

xi

Detail from Fig. 192

Kansas City, Missouri
An Architectural History
1826-1976

2

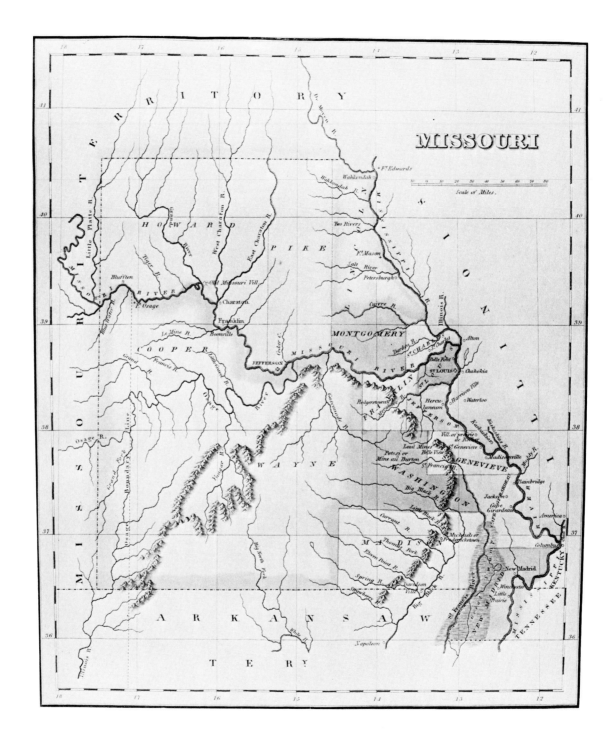

1826-1870
The Struggle for Identity

Kansas City's architectural history begins in 1826. In that year a flood forced the relocation of a small fur trading post. It was moved a few miles upstream from its original site on the south bank of the Missouri River. And it was at this new location that the city we know today as Kansas City, Missouri eventually developed.

The trading post was first established in 1821 by François Chouteau, a French fur trader, who was related to the Chouteaus of St. Louis. It was located in the vicinity of the bridge that now bears his name. Although the site is within the present corporate limits of Kansas City, Missouri, it was not so included until the annexations of 1909. While that trading post is significant as the place where the first permanent, non-native settlement began in the area, it did not survive for long.

When it was flooded out in 1826, Chouteau selected another location. It was this second site, near the south end of the ASB Bridge, which became the nucleus of the present city. Chouteau's establishment continued there despite later floods, and it soon attracted a number of settlers to the immediate area.

Chouteau's arrival in western Missouri happened to coincide with the state's admission to the Union in 1821. Understandably, the fur trading establishment was located so that it would be close to Indian and trapper clients and

accessible to river transportation. Upstream were the inner reaches of the continent. Downstream lay St. Louis and the markets beyond. In fact, Chouteau built on lands that were still reserved to the Indians in the new state. The site is readily identifiable on an 1822 map of Missouri (Fig. 1). It was situated on the south bank of the Missouri River, immediately east of the state line.

Soon after statehood was achieved, a trail to Santa Fe was developed by some central-Missouri entrepreneurs. Fort Osage, located some miles east of Chouteau's Landing, was a factor that brought the trail to the general area of what would soon be Jackson County. Initially the fort was a key station on the overland route. However, with the growth of trail-traffic and of settlements in western Missouri, there was a final removal of the Indians from the state in 1825. Soon thereafter Fort Osage was abandoned. Jackson County was organized in 1826-27 in the area south of the river along the state line. Independence, which was created as the county seat, became the principal staging and outfitting center for the wagon trains and it prospered.

Chouteau's trading post, which was located on the Missouri River just east of the confluence with the Kansas River, was some distance from Independence and the trail. The latter cut diagonally southwest across the county after leaving Independence. So for a number of years, Chouteau's Landing consisted of only a few log structures built by the fur traders, who were mostly French and not much involved in the developments generated by the trail. However, other

Fig. 1. GEOGRAPHICAL, STATISTICAL AND HISTORICAL MAP OF MISSOURI, 1822. (SC-UMKC)

settlers were entering the county. It was inevitable that a second staging area, for assembling and outfitting the wagon trains, would be established farther along the trail.

In 1835, near ample camp grounds and good water, and close to the state line, the town of Westport was platted to serve the Santa Fe trade. After a slow start, business grew, and Westport's success began to impact on Chouteau's river landing which lay four miles due north.

While it is not clearly delineated on the map in Figure 1, there is a great bend in the Missouri River where the Kansas or Kaw River, as it is commonly known, joins with it. Just beyond Kawsmouth, constricted by the terrain, the augmented Missouri River scoured its channel along the south bluffs. A rocky ledge at what would be the foot of Main Street served as a natural levee (Figs. 6 and 8). It was near there that Chouteau had rebuilt his warehouse, and it was to the landing that others had come.

We must remember that the lower portions of the Missouri River had been well traveled by traders and the military. By the 1830s it was a major trafficway across the state despite shifting channels and other obstacles to navigation. Downstream from Kawsmouth, the general flow of the Missouri is eastward to its junction with the Mississippi, a few miles north of St. Louis. However, above the Kaw the river's course is from the northwest. So here at Chouteau's Landing, or Westport Landing as it was called by some, where the great river changed direction, those who used it as the first leg to the west or southwest left the river. Four miles to the south of the landing lay Westport. There one could tranfer to the wagon trains.

Westport soon gained the advantage over Independence as a transfer point from river to trail. It had access to a much more convenient river landing, and its more westerly location cut at least a day off the trail time. Westport's growing prosperity, which increased with traffic on the trail, was reflected in developments at the landing. In 1839 a plat was prepared for the riverport, and the Town of Kansas came into being. Meanwhile, across the river, the Platte Purchase of 1836 opened up nearby lands between the old state line and the Missouri River to settlement. This was followed by the development of a trail to Oregon in the early 1840s.

With traffic generated by the Mexican War of 1846-48 and the discovery of gold in California in 1849, the two small communities of Westport and Kansas grew in importance and wealth. In response to these developments, the Town of Kansas was officially organized by the County Court in 1850. Three years later, the City of Kansas was finally chartered by the Missouri General Assembly. Common usage quickly converted that name to Kansas City, but this designation did not become official until 1889.

What did these two communities look like in their first flush of affluence? Neither was very large. One early commentator, Charles C. Spaulding, who may have inflated his figures, wrote that Westport had a population of 300 in 1846 and 1,500 in 1855. Kansas City had 700 residents in 1848. However, cholera, a frequent visitor to the river landing, reduced the population perhaps to 300 in 1851. But things improved, and despite the bloody Border Troubles, which stemmed from the issue of extending slavery into Kansas which was on the verge of statehood, both river and trail towns prospered. Soon, however, Kansas City became the dominant one of the pair. By the 1860 census, Kansas City had nearly 4,500 residents, and Westport 1,200. Clearly considerable progress had been made in the twenty-five years since the establishment of Westport had increased the importance of the landing on the river where Chouteau had relocated his warehouse.

Today, the site of old Westport can be found in the diagonal skew of the street grid where Broadway intersects Westport Road. That orientation was most likely determined by a small stream and a road bridging it. The latter, called Main Street in Figure 2, is now Westport Road. The crossing street at left center, called Main Cross Street, is now Pennsylvania. A short distance to the west of that intersection was the stream and a mill. Nearby were the residences, commercial structures and other facilities usual to a small town. We are told that in July of 1855 there were sixty-one commercial and craft houses, three hotels, two churches and three schools. There was housing for a population estimated at fifteen hundred. This information was provided by Charles

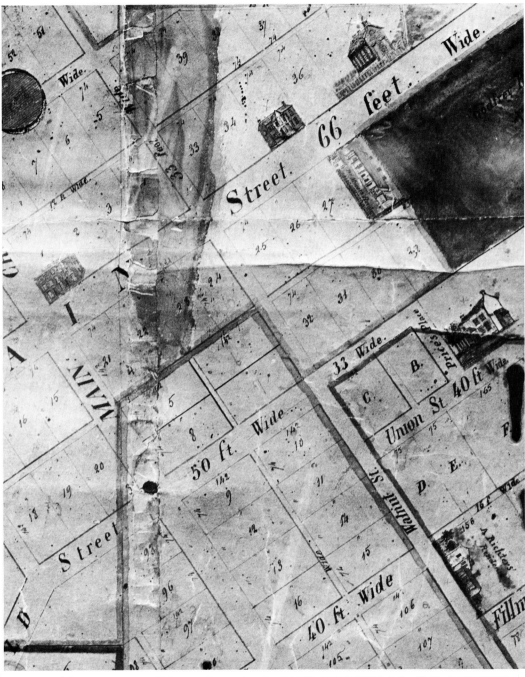

Fig. 2. Detail from SPAULDING'S MAP OF WESTPORT AND ADDITIONS, July, 1855. (MVR-KCPL)

C. Spaulding who also prepared a large map of Westport, from which is shown a detail in Figure 2. This portion includes a number of pictorial vignettes, one of which shows the leading hotel, the Harris House, located just above the "I" in Main Street.

From this 1855 city virtually nothing survives. A rare example, but happily preserved with few changes, is the Harris Residence of 1854-55 (Fig. 3). It has been moved a short distance from its original site, and twice it has been restored, most recently in 1970. It is now owned by the Westport Historical Society. The house is representative of the two-story brick style that many of the more affluent settlers built in the region. The principal block is five-bay with a central hall. The two-story galleried ell, that was an early addition, is a typical feature. Houses of this size and proportions lent themselves to the addition of Classic Revival details. For the most part, the 1850s buildings in the area were rather austere, stressing utility over appearance. The central hall plan is

6

Fig. 4. ALBERT G. BOONE STORE, 500 Westport Road. Built in the late 1840s, it received major remodeling between 1880 and 1892 when the step-gable and store front were added. The one-story section to the rear was added c. 1892-1904. (photo 1972)

Fig. 3. HARRIS RESIDENCE, 4000 Baltimore. Built in 1854-55 at the southwest corner of Main and Westport Road and moved to present location in 1922. (photo 1972)

typical, carried from Virginia to Kentucky and Tennessee, from where many of the settlers had come. Its usage goes back to the Colonial Period. Classic Revival features, if used, were concentrated on the principal facade, often in the form of a pedimented porch and in the door framing. However, Classic details often were rather freely adapted (Figs. 12 and 13). Sometimes there is only a hint of an entablature, and a doorway may approximate a Classic distyle-in-antis portico, such as that found in the Harris Residence.

The use of brick after the mid-1830s was common, but a good many of the early buildings were of log or frame construction. This is not surprising since northern Jackson County was then heavily forested. From what we have learned, these wooden buildings were generally simpler and more severe in their design treatment than were the brick buildings.

Commercial buildings in Westport were also simple and

practical. The austere facade of the Albert G. Boone Store (Fig. 4), though augmented and changed in several remodelings, is representative. It has the distinction of having been in continuous commercial use since the original portion (on the corner) was built in the late 1840s, replacing an earlier wooden store-building. Near the Boone Store, the Harris House Hotel stood until 1922. An old photo (Fig. 5) enables us to recognize its likeness on the Spaulding map (Fig. 2), and though the ground story is shown in its remodeled form in the photograph, we can see something of the blunt practicality of the 1848 design in the upper portions. Together, the Boone Store and the Harris House summarize the utilitarian design common in commercial architecture in this period, where the openings are unadorned and ornamental trim is at a minimum. The schools and churches in Westport apparently were equally severe, and most residences were undoubtedly little more than functional shelters.

The earliest roads from Westport to the river were whatever trails allowed the wagons to traverse the hilly terrain. By the end of 1858 a turnpike based on Kansas City's Grand Avenue became the principal road. Its establishment confirmed the growth of the river town that twenty years earlier consisted of, as one pioneer recalled, a clearing of a few acres on a high ridge which was connected to the levee by several deep gorges that served as roadways. In 1847 a wagon road had been cut through the bluffs at Main Street. The levee, which was the principal business street then, was widened and paved in 1855. Other improvements, such as the grading of other streets, followed.

The earliest view we have of Kansas City is preserved in two different illustrations. One, a wood engraving, appeared in *Ballou's Pictorial* of 4 August 1855. The other is a German etching published in 1853 (Fig. 6). This view shows a line of assorted structures stretched along the river, and several small houses on higher ground. Between the two buildings on the far right we can see the start of the Main Street cut. The bluffs outside of view, to the right, were much steeper than those shown in the etching. There is a close conformity between the two prints in such details as the architecture and principal terrain features. The etching is larger and has finer

detailing. However, there is considerable variation in the number, type and placement of vehicles, rivercraft, animals and people. This argues against one of the prints being based on the other, or both on a drawing of the town.

A daguerreotype original, on the other hand, would have presented the printmaker with the problem of inventing movable features since only the fixed elements were readily recorded by the long exposures then required. This argument for a photographic prototype for the prints is supported by a body of evidence that points to T. M. Easterly of St. Louis as the probable photographer. He is known to have made daguerreotypes of towns along the Missouri River, quite possibly in 1848, the year to which the view preserved in the print is dated.

What can we say about the appearance of the city in the last years of the 1850s? A lithographic view of the city purported to date to 1855 does not comport too well with a description of the city that was written a few years later. The pictorial version shows a levee more built up than the written

7

Fig. 5. HARRIS HOUSE HOTEL, originally on Westport Road at Pennsylvania, northeast corner. Built c. 1848 and later remodeled, it was demolished in 1922. (MC, MVR-KCPL)

8

DRAWN AFTER NATURE

KANSAS

Fig. 6. GERMAN ETCHING, with added color, showing Kansas City, Missouri, c. 1853. This view is presumed to have been based on a daguerreotype made c. 1848. (MVR-KCPL)

version records, and little else is available from this period on which to make an assessment. There are some things about which we can be certain. We know the basic geography of the town in that period. There was a row of commercial structures along the four blocks of the levee, from what today would be Wyandotte on the west to Grand (then Market) on the east. These ranged from wooden buildings, some of log construction, of no particular quality to multi-story brick buildings. Above the levee the bluffs rose rather precipitously near Wyandotte, cresting as much as one hundred feet above the waterfront. Several gullies cut the bluffs. These served as early roadways to the river and thus set the street grid that still obtains near the river. Only Main and Market Streets had been graded in 1857. Along these, near the levee, a number of buildings had been built.

On the crest of the bluffs, about Third Street, there were a number of structures, ranging from old homesteads to some commercial buildings. Others were scattered farther south.

The public square was located between Fourth and Fifth, and Main and Walnut, and it served as the site for a modest City Hall and a marketplace. Today, the old square forms the southwest quadrant of the present City Market. Beyond the square there were newer developments, concentrated along a corridor that focused first on Main and then along Grand through McGee's addition that took the city south to Twentieth Street in the 1859 annexation.

A detail taken from the first fully surveyed map of the city made in 1860 shows us a familiar street layout (Fig. 7). North of Second there have been enormous changes due to flood control measures and railroad construction. We can also see the shift of the street grid once we go past the line of Independence Avenue, and the disjunctions that still exist in the pattern of the streets in the downtown area. Today it is only the street grid and the public square that remain to link us to the ante-bellum river town.

As far as we can tell, all of the architecture built before the Civil War within the boundaries of that city, which were Twentieth Street on the south, the state line on the west, and Lydia on the east, is either gone, or the few remnants are radically modified. Also, no old photographs of the city or of individual buildings have been found which we can date with confidence to the period before the Civil War, though we know there were photographers working in the city. What early drawings exist tell us little more than that the terrain was hilly and that the buildings were small, plain and scattered. Some photographs taken soon after the Civil War do record pioneer buildings. From these and early structures elsewhere in Missouri, plus old descriptions, we can infer the appearance of the architecture a visitor would have found in the Kansas City of 1850s.

For example, an 1867 photograph (Fig. 8) gives us a fairly good idea of what the Gillis House Hotel looked like a decade earlier. We can see the blunt plainness which was good enough for the large, transient population that had little to choose from in the matter of hotel accommodations. But this represents the hotel remodeled and expanded at least once since it opened in 1849, and the companion commercial buildings shown in the photograph are probably post-war but we cannot be sure of this.

Another ante-bellum structure that was located in the old river town survived well into the twentieth century. This was the Frye P. McGee Residence built in 1848 (Fig. 9). It had deteriorated considerably prior to its demolition in 1955 to make way for new approaches to the ASB Bridge. Undoubtedly it had undergone numerous modifications over the years, but its basic, early characteristics stand out. It was a three-bay, two-story brick with a side hall, and stylistically it relates closely to the Harris Residence in Westport (Fig. 3). The two-story facade gallery seen in the photograph may or may not be original to the house. However, we know that such were built in the 1840s and 1850s. We can see one on the levee in the early view of the city already discussed (Fig. 6).

Other structures still standing in and around Kansas City fill in the gaps of our picture of the city in the 1850s. We know that many log structures were built ranging from churches and warehouses to individual cabins. By the time Chouteau reached Kawsmouth, it is unlikely that he would have used the upright-log construction known as *poteaux-en-terre* and introduced by French settlers in the Mississippi Valley in the mid-eighteenth century. Fort Osage, some

9

10

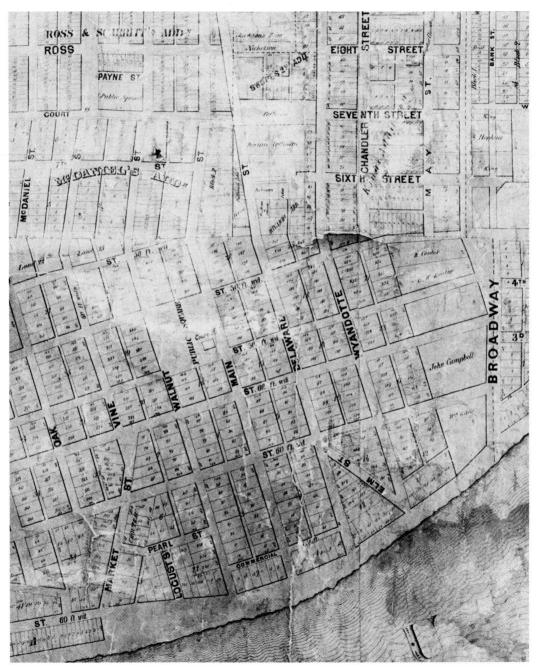

Fig. 7. Detail from O'FLAHERTY'S MAP OF KANSAS CITY, MISSOURI, 1860 (north at bottom of map). (SC-UMKC)

Fig. 8. GILLIS HOUSE HOTEL AND LEVEE, between Wyandotte and Delaware Streets in August, 1867. (NSC, MVR-KCPL)

twenty miles east, used horizontal notched logs. A small Catholic Church built by Father Roux near the landing was basically nothing more than a log cabin. Throughout the area, log buildings of all types were built, and a number survive. One of the largest is the Flintlock Church that was built originally in Platte County in 1848. It is now preserved in restored condition as part of Missouri Town 1855, at Lake Jacomo in Jackson County (Fig. 10). Stylistically, it is typical of nearly all log buildings in that utility and economy were paramount concerns.

12

Fig. 9. FRYE P. McGEE RESIDENCE, 513 E. Fourth. Built in 1848 and demolished in 1955. (photo 1955)

The Jacob Ragan Home (Fig. 11), which we know only from an 1886 photograph, was a two-story farm house with a one-story ell that gives the appearance of being a weatherboarded log structure. This practice became common in the area, and there may still be a number of undiscovered, early log houses within the city limits. The Ragan Home also shows a two-story, columned porch capped with a gable suggesting that the building which we see in the photograph dates to at least the mid-1850s, and that there was some attempt to work within the conventions of Classic Revival design. (See Figure 12 for comparison.)

More pretentious residences were designed and built in the region. It is interesting to note that many were farm houses, though urban examples can still be found in Independence and Lexington in good condition. The John B. Wornall House (Figs. 12 and 13) is the most impressive Classic Revival design to survive within the present city limits. Once the heart of a large farm south of Westport, it has been effectively restored as a museum house by the Jackson County Historical Society which now owns it. Constructed in 1858, it is an example of the central-hall, two-story house that was so popular in western Missouri before the Civil War. It makes a conscious attempt to follow Classic Revival design concepts. The facade is rigorously symmetrical, and there is a full entablature that goes around the entire house, though it is not correctly detailed. And there are four Doric pilasters on the facade that repeat the design of the prostyle portico, though the proportions and details are typically too tall and too arbitrary to be called accurate. All of this points to the hand of the contractor-builder rather than an architect. One can find similar designs in Kentucky, from where the Wornalls had come. The interior detailing is even less rigorously Classic. It reflects the growing freedom that one finds in what might be called the Carpenter-Classic style, particularly as the 1850s wind down. The use of brackets as part of the entablature is a common feature of this mode.

An interesting variation of this free-hand formulation of the Classic is the Alexander Majors House (Fig. 14). Built of wood in 1856, it has a T-plan in contrast to the more common ell of the Wornall House (Fig. 13). And the porch on the facade, which originally was two full stories, is recessed. It, too, has rather narrow proportions for the columns.

Here and there in the county, Gothic Revival cottages were built, both in brick and wood. Few survive, and a rare example in wood is the Archibald Rice House of 1844 (Fig. 15), which today lies just beyond the present city limits. It is clearly a carpenter's adaptation of a pattern book design. It also shows some awareness of the characteristics associated with the style as can be seen in the octagonal columns and their capitals, the scrollwork of the bargeboards, and the row of pendants below the gutters. There are also rectangular hood-moulds over the principal windows that further suggest the builder's awareness of more formal prototype designs.

On the Rice House property there is a small log cabin (Fig. 16) that is known as Aunt Sophie's Cabin. Reputed to date to the 1830s, it is typical of the one room cabin that was built all over the state, often as the first shelter for the pioneer. But it has another distinction; it was the cabin of a slave, and it reminds us that Missouri, even on the frontier, was a slave state. The Black population, slave and freeman, provided an important number of building craftsmen in the area, though the records on these, as might be expected, are very sparse. Since the majority of the Blacks were engaged in agriculturally related work, the architecture associated with them in the ante-bellum period has suffered the fate of the many farm buildings that lost their purpose as farms consolidated, and then were redeveloped into non-agricultural use.

As we study the early buildings of the area, it is evident that traditional practices and builder's memories of structures elsewhere—aided by the pattern books—are the sources for much of what deliberate styling can be found in the architecture of the 1840s and 1850s. We know that there were architects—by title if not training—in the young city. In all likelihood this designation merely meant that some builder was also prepared to provide some design work and supervision of the construction done by other craftsmen. It was unlikely that the title, in that period and place, meant that there had been special training in the art.

One finds that combined listings, as architect-builder or architect-carpenter, occurred. These reflect a usage common

Fig. 10. FLINTLOCK CHURCH, located originally off of US 71 about four miles north of Platte City in Platte County, now relocated to Missouri Town 1855 at Lake Jacomo, Jackson County. Built in 1848. (photo 1972)

Fig. 11. JACOB RAGAN RESIDENCE as it appeared c. 1886. A farmstead located at the northeast corner of Armour and Gillham Road. (NSC, MVR-KCPL)

13

14

Fig. 12. JOHN B. WORNALL RESIDENCE, northeast corner Wornall Road at 61st Terrace. Built in 1858 and now restored to that period. (photo 1972)

Fig. 13. JOHN B. WORNALL RESIDENCE, 61st Terrace view. (photo 1972)

16

Fig. 14. ALEXANDER MAJORS RESIDENCE, 8145 State Line Road. Built in 1856 with later additions and changes. (photo 1973)

Fig. 15. ARCHIBALD RICE RESIDENCE, 8801 E. 66th, Raytown,
Missouri. Built in 1844. (photo 1973)

ate cause, reflecting a southern origin for many residents and
a tradition of slave-ownership. This was countered, however,
by others, such as the large German population found in the
east-central section of Missouri. The differences were keenly
felt in Jackson County, which had previewed the Civil War in
the border troubles. It was not long before the county was the
scene of battle, martial law and considerable depredations.
Kansas City, which was turned into a Union outpost in an
area largely Confederate in its sympathies, suffered from the
war's effect. Population declined and property deteriorated.
In contrast, secure upstream towns such as Leavenworth and
St. Joseph prospered. But despite its wounds, Kansas City still
had the advantage of its location, and there was still the
potential of trade to the west and southwest. Also, there were
people of ambition and vision who saw Kansas City's future
in terms of it becoming a railroad center.

17

Fig. 16. AUNT SOPHIE'S CABIN, 8801 E. 66th, Raytown, Missouri. Built
c. 1830. (photo 1973)

elsewhere in the United States. Overall, the evidence presented by the older buildings, whether the Gillis House Hotel
or the Wornall House, is that prior to the Civil War the
formally trained architect was either not available or not in
demand. This may have begun to change about 1860. But
then the Civil War impacted on Jackson County, and Kansas
City's affairs took a significant downturn.

A goodly portion of Missouri's population, particularly
along the Missouri River, was sympathetic to the Confeder-

18

Fig. 17. THE KANSAS CITY BRIDGE, better known as the HANNIBAL BRIDGE, as it appeared August 2, 1869, shortly after its completion. Replaced in 1917. (SC-UMKC)

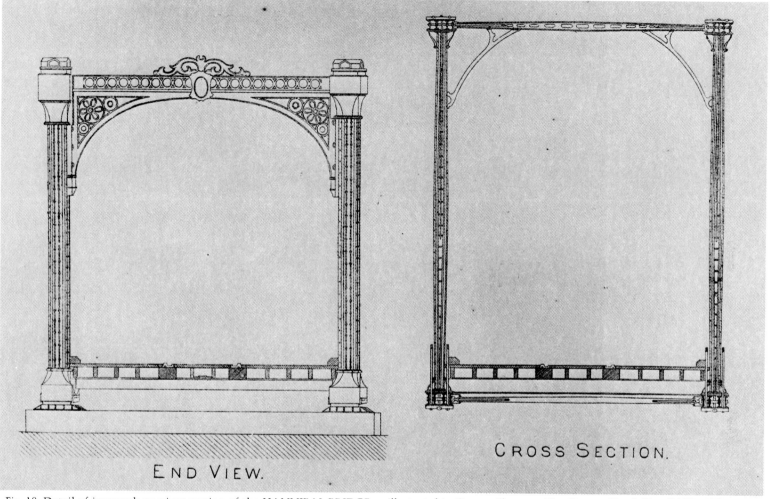

END VIEW.

CROSS SECTION.

Fig. 18. Detail of ironwork on pivot section of the HANNIBAL BRIDGE as illustrated in Octave Chanute, *The Kansas City Bridge* (1870). (SC-UMKC)

In 1860, Kansas City's population had reached nearly 4,500, about half of the number in St. Joseph. By the end of the Civil War this had dropped to perhaps 3,500, with many of these newcomers. But with peace declared, within a year or two the population had increased dramatically. One estimate for 1866 is 15,000, another for 1867 is 28,000. While these undoubtedly were off the mark, growth was sizable and swift. Much of this can be attributed to completion of a rail line to the east, when the Missouri Pacific's line, after considerable politicking, reached Kansas City's levee in 1865.

The following year, work began on the very first bridge to span the Missouri River. The completion of the Kansas City Bridge, better known as the Hannibal Bridge (Fig. 17), in the summer of 1869 provided a connection to the Hannibal and St. Joseph Railroad. Kansas City was soon fully committed to the railroads. The bridge was replaced in 1917. It is remem-

Fig. 19. MAIN STREET looking north from Sixth Street in 1868. (NSC, MVR-KCPL)

bered primarily for its engineering which was indeed a significant accomplishment under the direction of Octave Chanute. However, it also had some features of architectural interest. While it cannot be seen too easily in Figure 17, the vertical elements were ornamented, particularly in the pivot section. An illustration from Chanute's account of the building of the bridge (Fig. 18) permits us to see the amount of ornament that was used, and it reminds us of the fact that iron was being used more and more in architecture, both structurally and decoratively. (See Figures 22 and 24 for examples of the latter.)

In the few years between the end of the Civil War and the completion of the bridge, numerous changes occurred in the city. River traffic, which had been impeded by the war, was in the process of being replaced by the year-round reliability of the railroads. This process ensured that the river would lose its role as a focus for commercial activity. The city would no longer require the services of a Wharf Master by 1873, and the railroads would now be a factor in the location of commercial and industrial architecture, and in the placement of housing in the city.

As the city turned its back on the river, Main Street completely displaced the levee as the principal locus of business activity. An old photograph of Main Street, looking north from Sixth (Fig. 19), provides an interesting panorama of a boom town in 1868. A mixture of frame and brick buildings, a few reaching to three stories, and most with wooden sidewalk awnings, flank the street with its stone gutters. In the middle distance, on the right, there is a gap which marks the public square, with the City Hall, set back from Main, just barely visible. Here and there can be seen some evidence of architectural design for its own sake, with elaborate cornices or decorated window lintels. Stone, which was used extensively for foundations, was also used for trim, such as lintels and quoins, and rather rarely an entire facade might be done in stone (Fig. 21).

The streetscape preserved in the photograph is now completely gone. Except for the present buildings of the City Market, the portion of Main Street represented in Figure 19 is nearly devoid of architecture. However, Delaware Street, one

Fig. 20. PACIFIC HOUSE HOTEL, 401 Delaware Street. Rebuilt in 1868, Asa B. Cross architect. (photo 1973)

21

block to the west, which developed a bit slower than Main, retains a few of its late-1860s buildings.

The most interesting survivor is the Pacific House Hotel (Fig. 20), both because of its early importance as a hotel, and the fact that the original exterior remains. The building we see today is the 1868 rebuilding of an 1860 hotel of the same name which had burned in 1867. Asa Beebe Cross is credited as the architect, and the discipline of the facade, especially if compared to the Gillis House Hotel in Figure 8, does suggest a person with some training. Cross, who came to the city in 1858 from St. Louis, is supposed to have had some architectural office experience in his background, but in Kansas City he was initially in the lumber business. Some believe that from the first he provided architectural services as well, and that he did the 1860 design for the Pacific House. In any case, he was definitely involved in architecture by 1867. He soon gave up his connection with the lumber yard and continued as an architect until his death in 1894.

A notable feature of the Pacific House Hotel is that its

Fig. 21. COMMERCIAL BUILDING, 310 Delaware Street. Built 1866 or 67, the facade has been modified and also reduced in width. (photo 1974)

22

Delaware facade retains the early ironwork arcade of the ground story. The corbelled brick cornice is also unchanged. Both features were used on other buildings of the period (Fig. 30), though in most cases ground stories were later remodeled.

Another Delaware Street survivor from the late 1860s merits our attention, though in contrast to the Pacific House Hotel it is but a fragment of the original. This is the building at number 310 (Fig. 21). This design is unusual in that the entire facade, originally seven bays wide, was built of stone, including an arcaded ground story (Fig. 30). Sometime in the nineteenth century, for reasons not yet known, the four bays to the right were removed and replaced in the extension of another early structure. The truncation of the windows and the remodeling of the ground story appear to be later changes. Nevertheless, some of the sensitivity of the original design remains, such as the Classic treatment at the cornice level. This suggests that there might have been an architect's hand involved. One can find in old photographs similar cornice treatments fabricated in brick on commercial buildings in the district.

A building, long gone, which is fairly solidly attributed to an architect, once again Asa B. Cross, is Vaughan's Diamond of 1869 (Fig. 22). It occupied a key location at what was called The Junction, where Delaware and Main angled together at Ninth Street. An old photograph of the building provides a summary of the design vocabulary favored in the years when Kansas City was building its bridge and dreaming of greatness. The aggregation of assorted decorative details might be labeled simply as Victorian excess. But if one considers the unusual design problem generated by the narrow, triangular lot, one can see that there was an attempt to create a degree of monumentality for a facade that was to be a visual focus for the busy intersection of three, rather cluttered streetscapes. The solution, considering these limitations, is certainly competent for the period, and it does argue for some formal training for Cross. The use of the mansard roof is a case in point, and we begin to find it used more and more during the next two decades. Despite its once wide acceptance, the vagaries of demolition and renovation have removed almost all nineteenth century mansard-roofed buildings in the city, and, in fact, most of the buildings from the 1860s and 70s as well.

A factor contributing directly to the loss of much of the early, post-Civil War housing is the simple fact that many were located in what today are now business and industrial

Fig. 22. VAUGHAN'S DIAMOND at The Junction, at Ninth and Main, in 1871. Built in 1869, Asa B. Cross architect. (½ stereoscopic photograph, NSC, MVR-KCPL)

24

Fig. 23. MAJOR WILLIAM WARNER RESIDENCE, 1021 Pennsylvania. Built in 1868, renovated in 1966 for architectural offices by Monroe & Lefebvre. (photo 1974)

districts. Long ago they began to give way to commercial replacements. Those buildings that survived through nineteenth century city growth were typically in areas that had lost their early status. Consequently they were easily sacrificed by the planners of new highways and urban renewal projects that developed in the 1950s and 60s.

Quality Hill, in the vicinity of Tenth and Pennsylvania, had been prized by city leaders as a place to build their homes after the Civil War. But railroad and packing house developments in the neighboring West Bottoms, and upwind of Quality Hill, reduced its desirability, and decline slowly set in. By the end of World War II it was a prime target for urban renewal. It was one of the first areas in the city to come under that program. As a result, many fine old houses that might have been salvaged in the more sympathetic 1970s were lost in the 1950s and 60s. But some, particularly south of Tenth, were spared, and a few even have been renovated. One of the latter is the Major William Warner Residence of 1868, now

the offices for the architectural firm of Monroe & Lefebvre that did the preservation work (Fig. 23). It was not, however, completely restored to its original appearance. Missing are the one-story porch, which reached around the west and south sides—those seen in the illustration—and the entablature brackets, both common features in the post-Civil War period. It is no mansion, if measured by eastern models, but there is an expression of concern for some of the niceties of Victorian design which some other residences in the city, alas now gone, carried a bit farther.

We've labeled this long, formative period of Kansas City's architectural history "The Struggle for Identity." This designation recognizes the fact that Kansas City's roots are to be found in two frontier towns, and primacy had to be determined for one of them. It also acknowledges the struggle of the city to become a railroad center and thereby become the key city in the region, a struggle exacerbated by the impact of

Fig. 24. BROADWAY HOTEL, later the first COATES HOUSE HOTEL, southeast corner Broadway at Tenth, as it appeared in 1871. Completed in 1868, replaced 1889-91. Original 1857 design attributed to John Johnson, probably redesigned after the Civil War. (½ stereoscopic photograph, NSC, MVR-KCPL)

Fig. 25. View of KANSAS CITY in 1869, looking south from the top chord of the Hannibal Bridge. (SC-UMKC)

26

Fig. 26. Detail from RUGER'S BIRD'S-EYE VIEW OF KANSAS CITY, MISSOURI, 1869. (MVR-KCPL)

the Civil War. If there is one example that sums up the complexities of this period with all of the problems and difficulties faced by the young city—along with their successful resolution—it is the Broadway Hotel, later called the Coates House Hotel (Fig. 24).

It was planned in 1857, apparently by John Johnson, an English-born and trained architect who preferred to deal in Kansas City real estate rather than design buildings. Construction was halted by the Civil War when only the foundation walls had been built. These became part of a Union encampment at the Tenth and Broadway site. After the war, construction resumed, though whether there was a new design we do not know.

By 1868 the building was in use, and soon it was the fashionable hotel in town. The stone quoins and bracketed cornice are features common after the war, and so we can surmise some updating of the 1857 plans if not a completely new design. Unusual, regardless of whether it was designed before or after the war, is the great size of the hotel (compare to the Pacific House, Fig. 20) and its location, then some distance from the "center of town." These suggest a daring bit of speculation on the part of the first developers, a daring that helped the city survive the difficulties of the war years, to gain the railroads, and to enable the city to recover and grow after the war.

The construction anticipated the shift of the center of business activities to the south, a shift that was assisted by railroad development and a growth in population. As the community turned its back on the river, that was now bridged and whose levee now served the railroad as well as river craft, it would soon find the Broadway and Tenth location not too far south after all.

A view of the city, taken in August of 1869 from the top of the newly completed Kansas City Bridge (Fig. 25), shows us fragments of a raw city scattered over a hilly terrain, scarred with massive cuts through the bluffs, now to make way for the railroad rather than the wagons of yesterday. Off in the distance, to the right, anticipating the city that would build up to it, is the silhouette of the Broadway Hotel, itself perched on the edge of a ravine that in time would be filled in.

A detail of a bird's-eye view of the city, (Fig. 26), lithographed in 1869, gives another version of the scene. The evidence of old photographs tells us that the rendering of the form of the buildings is quite accurate. Thus we can read the view with some confidence. We still see a line of steamboats along the waterfront. Interposed between the river and the town is the railroad right-of-way that in time would become a more formidable barrier to the river than ever were the bluffs.

Business houses can be seen to be concentrated south of the square as well as north, making it clear that the river orientation of earlier times was in decline. With the city now committed to the railroads rather than the river or the wagon trails, the river bottoms would become new centers for development, for the railroads followed river grades when possible.

The attributes that once made Kansas City the paradigm of a frontier river town were being submerged. A new Kansas City, one that would be the railroad hub and regional merchandiser—with all of the attendant services and buildings that this required—was beginning to take its place. There was preparation for a growth in size and wealth that everyone was sure would come.

27

28

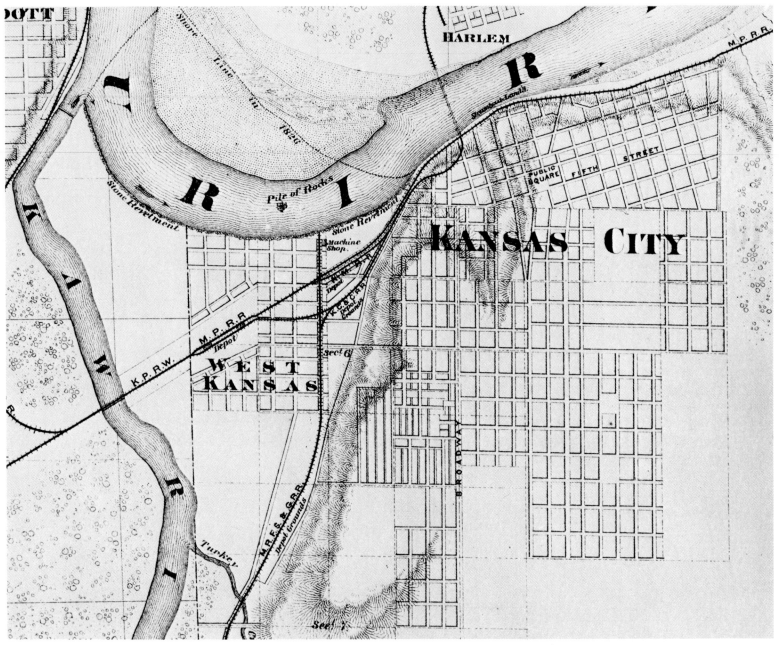

Fig. 27. Detail from MAP OF KANSAS CITY, MISSOURI, 1870. From Octave Chanute, *The Kansas City Bridge* (1870). (SC-UMKC)

1870-1910
Coming of Age

When Octave Chanute came to Kansas City in February of 1867 to become the chief engineer in the bridging of the Missouri River, the city had scarcely two years' experience with railroad service. Because the railroads used natural gradients wherever possible for their right-of-ways, trackage in the city concentrated in the flood plains (Figures 26 and 27). Consequently, the levee became the logical link that connected the railroads in the West Bottoms along the Kaw with those in the East Bottoms by the Missouri. The new bridge was primarily for railroad use, and it funneled its track to the West Bottoms via a deep cut at the western end of the levee (Fig. 25). By the time Chanute's work was done, it was inevitable that soon much of the West Bottoms would be committed to railroad use and to industry dependent on this service. In turn, this concentration became an influence on architectural developments as can be seen over the next several decades.

In 1868, Chanute had selected a site in the West Bottoms for the depot for the Kansas City & Cameron Railroad, the line which linked the city via the bridge to the Hannibal & St. Joseph Railroad. In this placement of a depot, he followed the lead of the Missouri & Pacific and the Kansas & Pacific Railroads that had built their depot and a hotel called the State Line House in the bottoms in 1867 (Fig. 27). A few years later, a union depot was built replacing Chanute's initial utilitarian structure.

Before the arrival of the railroads, the West Bottoms had been farm land. Now it provided the required space for the necessary shops, sidings, depots and freight houses which hopefully would be protected from floods by a stone revetment. Primary access to the bottoms was Bluff Street, which descended parallel to the line of the bluffs from its intersection with Fourth, Fifth and Sixth Streets just west of Broadway. Within a few years a horse-drawn street railroad on Fifth would provide, via Bluff Street, a public transit link between the Union Depot and downtown. The bottoms' industries also attracted residents to the area. Eventually a church and schools were built, though these and the residents would depart in later years.

Kansas City's rapid railway developments were not a localized phenomenon. They were linked to similar activities throughout Missouri. A considerable portion of the railroad construction in the State was stimulated by St. Louis' competition with Chicago for commercial primacy in the region of the upper Mississippi Valley. Kansas City's competition was different. Its struggle was against upstream cities such as Leavenworth and St. Joseph, and the location of a bridge over the river was seen as a key weapon in the resolution of that competition. When Kansas City won the bridge, it also acquired a notable advantage over its rivals. In addition to its link with St. Louis, it soon had a direct line to Chicago via Hannibal's bridge over the Mississippi, which was completed in 1871.

Also, Kansas City conveniently provided similar access for central Kansas and the greater Southwest. As a consequence of its growing network of railroads, Kansas City became the

30

funnel through which one could receive manufactured goods and could ship agricultural products, especially cattle, to either Chicago or St. Louis and thus to the entire eastern half of the United States. Kansas City also became a terminus for the cattle trade, and stockyards were built in the West Bottoms in 1870.

In the following year, the forerunner for what would be the Kansas City Union Stockyards was organized. This bi-state enterprise utilized a portion of the pinched-off peninsula of Kansas territory that had been created by an arbitrarily drawn state line and the looping course of the Kaw (see Figs. 27 and 39). Concurrently, the meat packing industry started in the same general area. In addition, grain elevators and flour mills were located in the bottoms to utilize the rail transport. Together, these various agribusinesses secured an economic base for the city that is still very important.

The peculiarities of the terrain, which had physically isolated the railway yards from the retail and commercial heart of the older city, now separated most of the new industrial and warehouse construction from the immediate area of the downtown. The spread-out character of Kansas City, which is so noticeable today, had its beginnings in the shift from the river to the railways, a reorientation that very much affected the city in the post-Civil War years.

The strong stimulus provided by the railroads was somewhat tempered, however, by a long period of rather unfavorable rate-schedules, a problem that plagued many communities after the Civil War. But even so, the city and the state grew rapidly in population. There was a significant influx of people into Missouri, both native-born and immigrant. The latter tended to settle more frequently in St. Louis than in Kansas City, and Kansas City did not acquire ethnic concentrations in the last decades of the nineteenth century of the sort and size that occurred in more eastern urban centers. In this respect, nineteenth century St. Louis was sociologically and culturally a more complex city. Its greater population, more diversified economy, with greater emphasis on man-

Fig. 28. MAP OF KANSAS CITY, MISSOURI, 1910, published by the Board of Park Commissioners. (MVR-KCPL)

Fig. 29. COATES OPERA HOUSE in 1871, northwest corner Tenth and Broadway. Started in 1869, dedicated in 1870, opened in 1871, remodeled in 1881, and destroyed by fire in 1901. (½ stereoscopic photograph, NSC, MVR-KCPL)

ufacturing, and its longer history, required and generated an architecture and architectural services more in common with eastern cities than was the case for Kansas City. Nevertheless, if Kansas City did not follow eastern characteristics and growth patterns in all respects, it aimed at achieving significant urban growth based on the logic of its location on the edge of the high prairies and as a distributing center for that region.

Growth required the creation of a great many city-provided services, as well as substantial physical changes in the community. The bluffs, hills and ravines, that created numerous obstacles to convenient traffic (Figs. 24 and 30), were challenged and subdued. By today's standards the tools

32

Fig. 30. View of KANSAS CITY, MISSOURI looking southwest from Second and Main. Photograph taken probably sometime between 1870 and 1872. (NSC, MVR-KCPL)

Fig. 31. COUNTY COURTHOUSE, northeast corner Second and Main. Photograph taken probably shortly after completion in 1872. Building destroyed by a tornado in 1886. (MVR-KCPL)

34

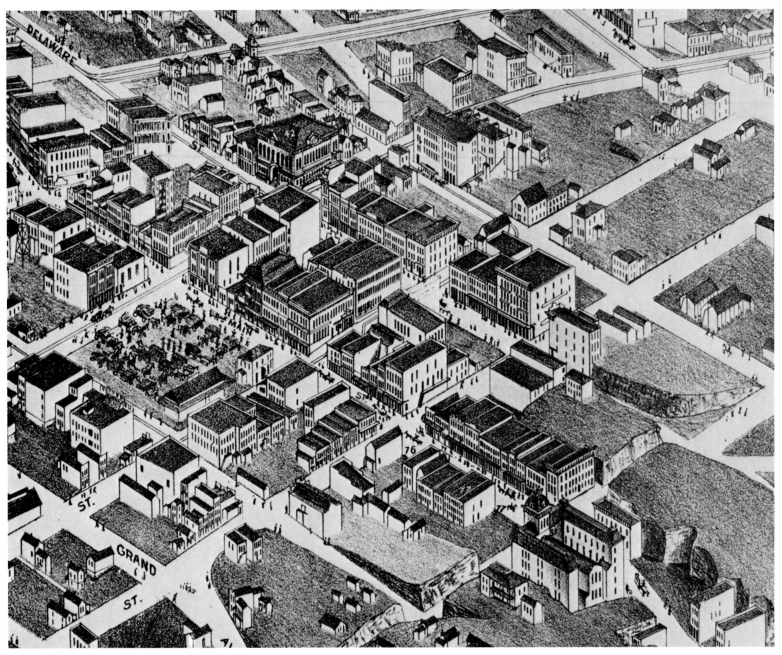

Fig. 32. Detail of public square area from RUGER'S BIRD'S-EYE VIEW OF KANSAS CITY, c. 1878. (MVR-KCPL)

and techniques were primitive indeed. But in the forty years of the period 1870 to 1910, bluffs were cut down by as much as sixty feet, hills leveled and ravines filled in. In the process, a boulevard and park system of genuine distinction was also created. While all of this was underway, the population was expanding ten-fold, to reach nearly a quarter of a million by 1910.

There was also a series of land annexations to incorporate this growth within city jurisdiction. The annexations in 1873 and 1885 had taken the city south to 31st Street and east to Cleveland, with the state line and the river remaining the other boundaries. Then in 1897 there were two sizable annexations, one reaching out to the east, and the other moved south to include Westport as part of Kansas City. Finally, in 1909 there was another large annexation. This took the city to 77th and 78th Street on the south. On the east the city extended just beyond the course of the Blue River. With this annexation, the city's area was increased to about sixty square miles (Fig. 28). This would remain the city's size until after World War II.

New city charters were required to cope with this growth. The Charter of 1875, the first since 1859, helped the city to deal with its fiscal needs and survive the depression that followed the Panic of 1873. The Charter of 1889 provided the governmental structure used until after World War I. It also provided for a change in name to Kansas City.

Growth required that the city provide appropriate services. Public education began in 1867. In the decade of the seventies, a number of schools were built. Also, during that decade a professional fire department was started, a public library created, a metropolitan police department organized, a waterworks constructed, and the Board of Trade was reorganized. Public transit was provided by a system of horse-drawn street railways.

If the Broadway Hotel/Coates House (Fig. 24) symbolized the recovery of the city after the Civil War, the Coates Opera House (Fig. 29), diagonally across the street from it, represented the ambition of the seventies. Started in 1869, the theatre, which was initially on the two upper floors, was dedicated the following year and became operational in 1871.

While the building exhibited no advances in design, the fact that a structure of this size and purpose was built is positive evidence that some city leaders had every intention that Kansas City become a city in appearance and appointments as well as in name. The original theatre interior was simple and fairly commodious. A decade later it would be upgraded with a remodeling that would also utilize the ground floor. In 1901 the Coates Opera House was destroyed by fire. By then, there were eight other theatres and concert halls in operation in Kansas City.

A view of the city, looking to the southwest from Second and Main and taken possibly as early as 1870 (Fig. 30), shows the Coates House Hotel and the Opera House just barely visible on the far left horizon. And as we move to the right, the distant panorama gives us a glimpse of Quality Hill. Just visible at the far right we see the great bend of the Missouri River. Left center, in the middle ground, we can see Delaware Street including number 310 (Fig. 21). Second Street cuts across the lower right, and we can see remnants of the bluffs that once carried across the entire area and which each year were further reduced down to street grade.

The city's rapid development in population growth generated a need for ready access to county offices. A Kansas City division of the County Court House was established at Second and Main. A hotel venture, which had failed before its intended completion in 1870, provided the opportunity. The unfinished hotel was sold to the county which converted it into a rather substantial courthouse structure. It opened in 1872. With its Second Empire styling (Fig. 31) it was without doubt one of the most fashionable buildings in the city, certainly far more impressive than either the Coates House Hotel or the Coates Opera House. A newspaper account called it the largest and costliest building in the county. It was destroyed by a tornado in 1886. We see a different view of it, this time from the rear, in a detail from an 1878 lithographed bird's-eye view of the city which looks to the southwest (Fig. 32). As we study this aerial image, which should be compared with Figure 30, we can see that the lithographer's draughtsman has recreated a market day, with wagons gathered in the public square to the north of the city hall identified as

35

Fig. 33. EXCHANGE BUILDING (BOARD OF TRADE), 502 Delaware. Built in 1877, Asa B. Cross architect. (photo 1972)

36

number 32 in the print. Both Main Street and Delaware can be seen to be important commercial streets. On the latter the recently completed Board of Trade Building, identified as number 42, stands as a substantial sign of commercial progress, four-square on its corner at Fifth Street. It still stands today (Fig. 33), somewhat altered from the 1877 design by Asa B. Cross, but it is still easily recognizable. The panel brickwork, the use of iron columns on the principal facade, and the rusticated basement story are representative of the rather individualized designs of what today we call the High Victorian, a period that also produced the sometimes personalized excesses of the style that is labeled Queen Anne. The loss of the old Board of Trade's ornamental cornice, its portico and other embellishments has reduced the effect of the original design. But the sturdy, four-story structure was a major addition to a city that was working hard to transform itself from the image that it presented ten years earlier (compare with Fig. 19).

To the south of Main Street, there was a solid stretch of commercial buildings reaching past Ninth Street. Most were three stories in height. An old stereoptican view, dated 1872, of a few of them on the east side of the 600 block (Fig. 34) is pictorially eloquent of a growing architectural awareness on the part of both client and practitioner in the years when the railroads impacted on the city. Regrettably, we cannot as yet assign designer's names to any of the four. We might be able to attribute the one on the far right to Asa B. Cross, for it is remarkably close in feeling to Vaughan's Diamond (Fig. 22). We can probably date it to about the same time, 1869, or soon thereafter. As far as we can tell, Cross was the recipient of most of the commissions in the 1870s which required the services of an architect. In the seventies he had little competition, for in this decade few others listed themselves in the City Directory as architects. On the basis of style, one can accept the possibility that Cross might have also designed the two buildings on the left in Figure 34, if we consider the way decorative window arches and cornices were used. But the Gothic design, the one behind the street light, seems far removed from all we know of Cross's style.

If we review the short list of other known architects of the period to whom no buildings as yet have been attributed, one possibility is William Reincke. While we have no solid evidence to support this assignment, it is apparent that a trained person prepared the design. We know that William Reincke came to Kansas City as Octave Chanute's chief draughtsman during the building of the bridge. By 1869 he listed himself as an architect and continued to do so through 1871 when he left the city. Whether he was any better trained, or more experienced in "modern styles" than the few other architects in the city, we do not know. But a design of this sort is so much more daring, and in fact so advanced for Kansas City, that it must have been the work of a transient such as Reincke. We do not see this sort of complexity again until the end of the decade, when a new group of architects came into the growing city.

The city was affected by the Panic of 1873. It was not until

Fig. 34. EAST SIDE OF MAIN STREET, from Sixth to Seventh, in 1872. (½ stereoscopic photograph, NSC, MVR-KCPL)

Fig. 35. OLD ST. PATRICK'S CATHOLIC CHURCH with parish house, 800 Cherry. Church attributed to Asa B. Cross, 1874-75. (photo 1977)

38

it obtained a new and more authoritative Charter in 1875 that the city was able to take some effective strides toward recovery. The difficult economic times affected the entire nation and it probably contributed to the decline in the number of people in the mid-1870s who were advertising themselves as architects in Kansas City. In the city and elsewhere the profession had virtually no regulation, and movement in and out of the field was influenced by the demand for architectural services.

Without doubt, it was Cross's already long tenure in the city that enabled him to continue his practice in the middle-seventies. He received several commissions during this period, some of which are still standing. One of these is a church, Old St. Patrick's Catholic Church, which is dated to 1874-75 (Fig. 35). The design work is characteristic of what we know of him, and we can assume he might have designed the Parish House to the immediate south, built c. 1878 (Fig. 36). This attribution is supported by the long-held conviction that he also remodeled for Seth Ward an ante-bellum house

Fig. 36. PARISH HOUSE of old St. Patrick's Church, 806 Cherry. Architect possibly Asa B. Cross, c. 1878. (photo 1977)

in 1871 (Fig. 37). If we compare the detailing of the porches of the two buildings, we can see a similarity that must be more than coincidence. But then we must acknowledge that this type of wood-working was not unusual at that time. The chronology of the Ward House is complex, and the facade appears to combine 1850s' elements with a good many later additions. The resulting appearance is really a far better expression of High Victorian taste than of the Classic Revival

Fig. 37. SETH E. WARD RESIDENCE, 1032 W. 55th. Original portion, 1856-57. Remodeling and additions, 1871/72. Attributed to Asa B. Cross. (photo 1977)

40

Fig. 38. QUINLAN-SNIDER RESIDENCE, 1005 Forest. Built c. 1876. Demolished. (MC, MVR-KCPL)

period to which a portion of the house probably dates.

The remodeled Ward House and the St. Patrick's Parish House can be taken as representative of the detached house in Kansas City in the seventies. On the other hand, the Quinlan-Snider Residence (Fig. 38), which was built in 1876 or soon thereafter, was atypical, at least in Kansas City at that time. The elaborate design, with its tower and ornate detailing, influenced by Second Empire styling, and the size of the house indicate the return of prosperity to the city. It also suggests a trained architect. Possibly it was someone like Edmond J. Eckel, a graduate of the Ecole des Beaux-Arts who settled in St. Joseph in 1869, where he then had a productive career. The Quinlan-Snider Residence was one of the most ambitious designs built in Kansas City in the seventies. In other cities, which either prospered during the Civil War or at least held their own, such Reconstruction Period residences were more common. But in Kansas City, that was a far more pretentious house than usual for that time. The house is now long gone, as are all the other residences of that genre from the seventies. Their age, size and location became negative factors in the matter of their preservation.

In keeping with the city's progress in the late 1870s, developments went forward in the West Bottoms, where the railroads, stockyards, packing houses, mills and elevators were concentrated. Another detail from the 1878 bird's-eye view (Fig. 39—compare with Fig. 32), shows us the West Bottoms and the new Union Depot, which had been built in 1878 to replace Chanute's simple structure on the site. It can be seen adjacent to the bluffs in the center of the illustration. Two years later, the Victorian Gothic structure was remodeled to serve increased traffic. The "new" station (Fig. 40), with its fussy, eclectic details was built parallel to the through-tracks that were located between the bluffs and the station. Across from the station, on Union Avenue, there was a crowded row of commercial buildings jammed into a triangle of land flanked by railroad tracks. The growth of passenger traffic in and out of the city was concentrated at this station, though others were built in the city. It was not too long before the constricted site and the arrangement of the tracks became limiting factors in expanding the station.

What little could be managed was primarily at the lateral ends of the 1880s building.

The station, with its cluttered exterior that fused fashionable Second Empire features with somewhat antiquated Gothic details, was, in fact, fairly impressive when it was built for a city of less than 60,000 population. But in 1900, with a population in excess of 160,000, the station proved inadequate for the city. The inadequacy could not be rectified despite a renovation effort by Van Brunt & Howe in 1898. This depot, however, continued to serve as the city's principal passenger station until late in 1914, when the new Union Station at Main and Pershing replaced it.

Today, the site of the old station is clearly visible in the cleared area just east of Union Avenue where it parallels the bluffs. All of the old commercial buildings that once faced it across Union Avenue are gone. The problem at the old station site was more than physical limitations on expansion. In 1881, a major flood shut down rail services for forty days. Though this did not deter further developments in the West Bottoms, the potential of flood-interrupted service and the implications of the crowded station-site were persuasive arguments for the eventual relocation of the station. This decision was accelerated by the devastating flood of 1903.

There were other dangers in the city beside floods. One of the most critical was the ever present hazard of fire, a matter very much in people's minds after the great Chicago fire of 1871 and the one in Boston the following year. The concern for fire prevention along with a need to start monitoring sanitary hookups to a sewerage system led to city supervision of construction to ensure health and safety in the city. Sometime between 1875 and 1880, a building code was enacted. While the restraints were mild at first, this was apparently the first governmental attempt to introduce some sort of control over architecture in the city. By 1909, for all practical purposes a modern code was in effect. In the intervening years, the city went through two major periods of construction, one peaking in the second half of the 1880s, the other in the very early years of this century, around 1906. It was also in this period of the late nineteenth and early twentieth century that professionalism in the practice of

41

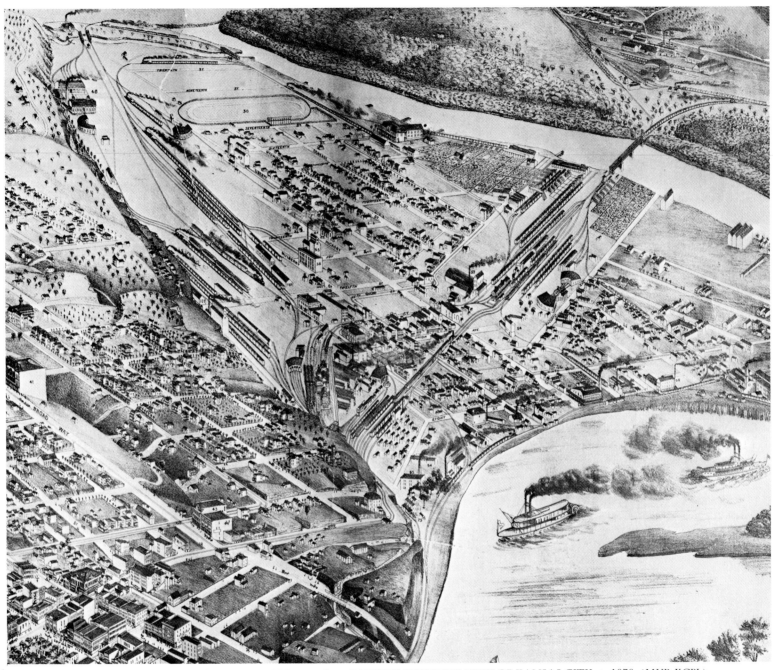

Fig. 39. Detail of WEST BOTTOMS and QUALITY HILL areas from RUGER'S BIRD'S-EYE VIEW OF KANSAS CITY, c. 1878. (MVR-KCPL)

Fig. 40. UNION DEPOT, on Union Avenue. Built in 1878, remodeled in 1880. Photo taken between 1880 and 1885. (½ stereoscopic photograph, MVR-KCPL)

In keeping with this growth, the federal government constructed a combined Post Office, Customs House and Federal Courts Building in a variant of the Renaissance style. It was completed in 1884 (Fig. 41). By the next year, 1885, the city was the scene of a building boom that received additional stimulation from the activity of outside investors. It was also in this year that the Boston architectural firm of Henry Van Brunt and Frank M. Howe opened an office in Kansas City. Two years later the firm made Kansas City its permanent home. By 1887, the population was about 125,000, well over double that of 1880. Taller buildings were being planned or built. Major outside firms, such as Burnham & Root of Chicago and McKim, Mead & White of New York City, opened temporary offices in the city.

The city's appearance was changing under the influence of prosperous times. There was increased architectural sophistication on the part of both practitioner and client. All of this combined to make over what had been, for all practical

43

architecture became firmly established in the city, though, in fact, one did not need formal training in order to set oneself up in practice. Architects ranged from those who were well trained professionals to those who were carpenter-builders, who simply proclaimed themselves, sometimes temporarily, architects.

The decade of the 1880s proved to be architecturally important to the city, both because there were more professionally competent architects working in the city, and because some significant buildings were erected. It was also in this decade that public transportation, in the form of street railways, which had been introduced in the seventies began to prosper. In 1885 the cable-car began replacing the horse-car. In time the city would have the third largest cable-mileage in the country, exceeded only by those of Chicago and San Francisco. The growing ease of movement within the city encouraged the development of the recently annexed areas.

Fig. 41. OLD FEDERAL BUILDING, 911 Walnut. Completed 1884, later Fidelity Bank, demolished 1929. From Whitney, *Kansas City, Missouri,* (1908). (SC-UMKC)

purposes, a medium-sized, western city just barely removed from its frontier origins. In keeping with this modernization, an electric power and light company was organized in 1886. In the following year a second Missouri River bridge was authorized but not then built. Then the bubble burst. The real estate boom collapsed in mid-1888. By 1892 construction activity was severely depressed. But before the decline set in, a great deal had been accomplished.

Seven buildings by the firm of Burnham & Root were

44

Fig. 43. BOARD OF TRADE BUILDING, 210 W. Eighth, later Manufacturers Exchange Building. Built in 1888, Burnham & Root (Chicago) architects. Demolished 1968. Photogravure from *Kansas City and Vicinity* (1900). (SC-UMKC)

Fig. 42. WILLIAM CHICK SCARRITT RESIDENCE, 3240 Norledge. Built in 1888, Burnham & Root (Chicago) architects. (photo 1973)

erected in the years 1887 and 1888. Several of the buildings were what Frank Howe would later call "first class." It is sad to report that only one of the seven still stands. This is the William Chick Scarritt Residence (Fig. 42). Root was the principal designer for the firm, and this house illustrates both his reliance on designs by men like Richard Morris Hunt and Henry Hobson Richardson, and his own independence and originality. The solid, rusticated stonework, the massive proportions, and the silhouette are related to Richardson. The flattened arches and the ornament on the tower suggest Hunt. But the house is not simply an imitation. There is a more open, more inviting quality than that found in similar

Richardson buildings, and there is little of the academicism found in Hunt's work.

A similar dependence—independence can be found in what was Burnham & Root's finest design for Kansas City, and one of their notable buildings regardless of location. This was Kansas City's second Board of Trade Building (Figs. 43 and 44). It was a competition design, one of the few held in the city, and it provided a real challenge to the architects. Provision for a large exchange room marked by the large arcaded windows in the left wing, adequate light and circulation for a large number of rental offices, and efficient traffic flow within the large building required an imaginative solution. While it is true that the fenestration and the tower, along with the interaction of the brick and terra cotta of the walls was dependent on Richardson's influence, the bold use of an exterior light court, the rich and playful detailing of decoration, most readily apparent around the central door (Fig. 44), were John Wellborn Root at his best. The ornament

Fig. 45. AMERICAN NATIONAL BANK BUILDING, northwest corner Delaware and Eighth. Built in 1888, Burnham & Root (Chicago) architects, demolished. (photo 1954)

Fig. 44. ENTRANCE, BOARD OF TRADE BUILDING, 210 W. Eighth. (photo 1954)

was more elaborate than that found in Richardson's work. It seemed far better controlled and more effectively used on the exterior than that which Louis Sullivan designed at that time. The design of the Board of Trade Building was clearly related to Burnham & Root's contemporary Rookery Building still standing in Chicago. Its demolition in 1968 was a severe loss not only to Kansas City's architectural wealth but also to American architecture in general.

The American National Bank Building designed by Burnham & Root of Chicago (Fig. 45) for a more conventional purpose invites comparison to a major work by the firm of Van Brunt and Howe of Kansas City, namely the Emery, Bird, Thayer Company Store, 1889-90 (Fig. 46). Both structures were brick with terra cotta ornament. Both have been demolished and with them a considerable portion of the city's history has been erased. The tightly composed bank building presented two slightly different facades on the somewhat wedgeshaped corner lot. This no doubt was a

46

Fig. 46. EMERY, BIRD, THAYER COMPANY STORE, Eleventh Street, Walnut to Grand, north side. Built 1889-90, Van Brunt & Howe architects. Demolished 1972-73. Northwest corner Eleventh and Grand. (photo 1972)

Fig. 47. CALVARY BAPTIST CHURCH, 1006 E. Ninth, later COVENANT BAPTIST CHURCH. Built in 1888, Edbrooke & Burnham (Chicago) architects. Reconstructed with some exterior deletions in 1949. (photo 1974)

48

Fig. 48. ST. MARY'S EPISCOPAL CHURCH, 1307 Holmes. Built in 1888, William Halsey Wood architect (New York City). (photo 1977)

Fig. 49. DAVID T. BEALS RESIDENCE, 2506 E. Independence. Built c. 1885, demolished. (MC, MVR-KCPL)

response to the two different street slopes and widths, and an elevated streetcar line that complicated the Eighth Street frontage. The isolated but richly detailed ornament, typical of Root, provided strong accents to the disciplined fenestration.

The site and plan of the store for Emery, Bird, Thayer Company presented an analogous problem, though it was built on a much larger lot and faced three streets on its sloping site. Each facade of the EBT Store was different in length, and each was individually composed. The size and location of the building, which affected one's view of the building, was a factor in this design. It was, of course, impossible to see the opposite Walnut and Grand facades simultaneously. The narrowness of Eleventh Street made it impossible to see that facade in its entirety, except from a raking angle. Consequently, the building was perceived as two corner views, and Figure 46 illustrates the most impressive of the two. Unification of the large and visually discontinuous exterior came from the strong horizontals created by the bands of ornament and the sidewalk-level open arcade. Also, the repetition of large, arched groupings of windows, similar to those on the exchange wing of the Board of Trade, and the type and placement of the ornament, related to both the Board of Trade and the bank building, provided for an integration of the exterior elements of the store building, and suggest the importance of Burnham & Root's work as an influence on the Kansas City firm. Van Brunt & Howe's office was eclectic in its design work, and while the Emery, Bird, Thayer Company Store was not especially innovative or particularly stylish for that matter, it was a large and solid statement in a design vocabulary that had produced some significant architectural masterpieces in the hands of its most gifted practitioners.

Another structure that shows a similar facade treatment is the Calvary Baptist Church, now the Covenant Baptist Church (Fig. 47). A design of the Chicago firm of Edbrooke & Burnham, who are perhaps best known for their design of the Georgia State Capitol (1884-89), the Kansas City church, of 1888, is Romanesque in contrast to the Georgia Statehouse which is academically Classical. The church underwent

Fig. 50. RESIDENCE, 1836 Pendleton. Built in 1888, Harry Kemp architect. (photo 1972)

49

Fig. 51. COATES HOUSE HOTEL, 1005 Broadway. South half (right) 1886-87, north half 1889-91, Van Brunt & Howe architects. (photo 1973)

reconstruction in 1949 after a fire and lost a steeply pitched and stone-gabled roof as well as a steeple on the tower. However, the excellent stonework of the lower stories remains intact and contrasts to the brick of the Romanesque buildings discussed earlier. It presents a far richer texture and appearance, even in its truncated condition, than does another church of that time, St. Mary's Episcopal Church (Fig. 48), by the New York architect, William Halsey Wood. The latter building, with its simple Gothic design in brick, is a striking contrast to the Baptist church. The two give us

some idea of the variety of work being done in Kansas City, and they remind us of the promise of enlarging opportunities that attracted outside architects to serve the city's needs. The number of architects listed in the City Directories tripled in the five years, 1884 to 1888, from twenty-two to sixty-five. There were seventy-two listed in 1889. This nineteenth century peak would not be reached again until 1904-05.

The designers for domestic architecture and their work varied even more widely than in the case of churches or commercial buildings, and we are hardpressed to identify

Fig. 52. NEW ENGLAND BUILDING, 112 W. Ninth. Built in 1887-88, Bradlee, Winslow & Wetherell (Boston) architects. (photo 1973)

50

sometimes, but not always and not regularly, listed themselves as architects. These people must have produced innumberable commercial designs as well as residences. However, it seems clear that the major design opportunities went to the established architectural firms, typically partnerships between trained architects, such as Henry Van Brunt and Frank M. Howe.

It was this firm that received the commission to extend and rebuild the old Coates House Hotel in a two-part project that saw a south wing of new design built in 1886-87, and a complete reconstruction of the old building to match in 1889-91. The result was the finest hotel of its time in Kansas City. In Figure 51 we see it long after its days of glory, but the exterior changed very little over the years. The belvederes that capped the corner pavilions are gone as is a wing for service people and support facilities that was at the rear of the main block. The interior, on the other hand, has lost virtually all aspects of the splendor that once made it the hotel of presidents. In January of 1978, a devastating fire destroyed the south portion of the hotel and claimed many lives. The future of the remainder of the building is, at this writing, uncertain.

As the new south wing of the Coates House Hotel was being completed, work began on the New England Building not too far away, at Ninth and Wyandotte (Fig. 52). Designed by the Boston firm of Bradlee, Winslow & Wetherell, its Renaissance-influenced design was complemented by its near neighbor to the east, the New York Life Building by McKim, Mead & White (Fig. 53). It was completed in 1890 two years after the New England Building. The disciplined terra cotta ornament and brickwork of the upper facades of the New York Life (Fig. 54) provide an interesting contrast to the richly textured stonework of the New England. Both herald the growing interest in Classicism that was so effectively demonstrated at the World's Columbian Exposition in Chicago in 1893. The ornament of the New York Life Building is particularly expressive of this design mode that provided an alternative to the pervasive influence of Richardson's Romanesque, though the grouping of the windows is indebted to that master architect.

architects for many of the homes. The David T. Beals Residence (Fig. 49) of c. 1885, for example, may have been designed by a Chicago architect, since the owner was from Chicago, and his imposing house was completed soon after his arrival in Kansas City. It no longer stands. It contrasts strongly with a large and exuberant Queen Anne design (Fig. 50) of 1888. The latter was the work of the architect Harry Kemp who apparently came to the city in that year to take advantage of the building boom. He was one of the many who left when the boom collapsed.

While some homes were architect-designed, many more appear to have been the work of contractor-builders who

Fig. 53. NEW YORK LIFE BUILDING and view of north side of the 100 block of west Ninth Street, with the KANSAS CITY DIME MUSEUM, No. 110 (now John S. Marshall Co.); the LYCEUM BUILDING, No. 104; the BUNKER BUILDING, No. 100 (also 820 Baltimore). NEW YORK LIFE BUILDING, 20 W. Ninth, McKim, Mead & White (New York City) architects, 1888-90. (photo 1973)

Fig. 54. Detail of upper stories of east wing of the NEW YORK LIFE BUILDING. (photo 1976)

A general change to Renaissance or Classic forms did not occur abruptly in Kansas City. Local architects moved cautiously in the matter of following the lead of the New York Life Building, though in time the latter would prove to be an important influence. As evidence of the caution we can cite two locally designed government buildings which were built during the construction slowdown of the 1890s. These are the City Hall of 1891, by Simeon E. Chamberlain (Fig. 55) and the County Courthouse of 1892 (Fig. 56) usually given to Asa B. Cross. Both were fussy variants of the Richardsonian Romanesque style, with no especially outstanding features. In contrast, the Federal Courts Building and Post Office that was built in 1896-1900, ending government use of the 1884 design (Fig. 41), was a miniature, late-nineteenth century statehouse (Fig. 57). A typical government building with its

52

Fig. 55. CITY HALL, southeast corner Main and Fourth. The second CITY HALL built 1890-91, Simeon E. Chamberlain architect. Demolished 1938. (NSC, MVR-KCPL)

Fig. 56. COUNTY COURTHOUSE, Missouri Avenue, north side Oak to Locust. Built in 1892. (MC, MVR-KCPL)

Renaissance dome and its free adaptation of Classic forms, the Federal project was very grand indeed, and stylistically more up-to-date than the local designs. Its interior space was severely criticized in later years, and it was demolished in 1937 to make way for the present Federal Courts Building (see Fig. 116). The City Hall and the County Courthouse were also demolished after the present buildings were built in the 1930s (Figs. 110 and 112). Of the three late nineteenth century buildings, the City Hall can claim the most notable feature: the innovative use of caissons. Louis Curtiss, an architect we will have occasion to mention again, was involved in that job of engineering.

In many ways, however, the most notable design achievement of the 1890s was the park and boulevard system which had been designed by George Kessler and constructed under his supervision. The first park board in the city was formed in 1890, the same year coincidently that a chapter of the American Institute of Architects was organized in Kansas City. Kessler's report on the park and boulevard needs for the city was released in October of 1893. By 1895, work on this ambitious plan was underway despite considerable opposition. By 1900 effective resistance to the plan had ceased. The map published by the park board in 1910 (Fig. 28) indicates the growth the system had achieved in that year. It also noted the additions that were planned. By 1915 the park and boulevard system, as it was to stand until after World War II, was virtually complete. Kessler, who had German training and a brief experience with Frederick Law Olmsted, came to the Kansas City area in the mid 1880s. With the design for what is now called Hyde Park, the area from 36th to 39th along Gillham Road, he made his mark as a landscape architect in the city. His plan converted a rugged hollow, privately purchased, into a new, high-priced residential section. Additional private design work followed, and this led to his employment by the park board. The rest is truly notable history.

His plan for the city was a bold and effective demonstration of the concept of the "City Beautiful." The conversion of blighted bluffs and ravines into parks, which were linked by a boulevard system of considerable extent, presented a model to be emulated by others. The plan was intended to affect the placement and design of buildings, and it indeed worked that way. Under these circumstances, Kansas City was ready to enter the new century with an optimism in outlook that ensured progress despite the depression that had followed the collapse of the real estate boom and the Panic of 1893.

The construction of a public library by the school board, which also included their offices in 1895-97 (Fig. 58), was another symbol of the intention to make Kansas City a major city. The design was by William F. Hackney, who had come to the city from Des Moines, Iowa, (where he had worked on the statehouse) in conjunction with Adriance Van Brunt (no near relation to Henry Van Brunt). The new library building was a clear commitment that the Renaissance style was going to be an important part of the design vocabulary for local architects. Working with Hackney was Charles A. Smith, who previously had been his draughtsman and who would take over Hackney's practice when the latter died in 1899. Smith had one of the longest and most productive architectural careers in Kansas City. We will come back to him again.

Elsewhere, utilitarian buildings were designed with far less concern for stylistic fashion. Even so one can see some awareness of style for style's sake in all but the meanest of buildings. And one can see that there were adaptations and changes over the years in design preferences. A group of commercial and warehouse buildings along Twelfth Street in the West Bottoms—officially the Central Industrial District—is a notable streetscape that has survived virtually unchanged since the end of the nineteenth century (Fig. 59). The individual designs are not especially outstanding, but the two-block range has a monumentality that is genuinely impressive. Some late nineteenth century residential streetscapes have also retained their appearance over the years. The work of real estate developers, who then as now were the principal agents in filling in the expanded city, can be seen throughout the older sections of the city. Some areas document the type of solid, middle-class housing that was popular at the end of the nineteenth and at the start of the twentieth century. The row of detached houses in the 500 block of Bellefontaine, erected in 1890, is a case in point (Fig. 60).

54

Fig. 57. FEDERAL BUILDING, east side of Grand, Eighth to Ninth. Second Federal Courts Building and Post Office, built 1896-1900, demolished 1938. (NSC, MVR-KCPL)

56

Fig. 58. OLD PUBLIC LIBRARY, 500 E. Ninth. Built 1895-97, William F. Hackney with Adriance Van Brunt architects; north addition 1917-18 by Charles A. Smith. (photo 1973)

Fig. 59. View of north side of the 1300 and 1400 BLOCKS OF WEST TWELFTH STREET. Commercial and wholesale buildings, 1879-1900. (photo 1974)

58

Fig. 60. RESIDENCES, west side of 500 Block of Bellefontaine. Built in 1890. (photo 1974)

While such construction did slow down in the later nineties, recovery in the next decade produced some significant increases in building and some striking changes in the urban landscape.

This recovery can be seen in a number of statistical indices. Population grew by 54% in the first decade of the twentieth century, from 163,752 in 1900 to 248,381 in 1910. And these people needed housing and places to work. The area of the city was significantly increased, first by two large annexations in 1897, which included Westport. Then in 1909 there was another substantial annexation, bringing the city's area to nearly 60 square miles. It was nearly four and one-half times larger than in 1885. The increase in construction needs was paralleled by an increase in the number of architects who were listed in the classified section of the City Directories, from 35 architects in 1894 to 102 in 1910.

The decade of the 1900s is noted for some fine work in both residential and commercial architecture. In the latter category, the changes wrought in the downtown skyline are

Fig. 61. R. A. LONG BUILDING and view of Tenth Street looking west from Grand. R. A. Long Building, northwest corner Grand & Tenth. Built in 1906, Howe, Hoit & Cutler architects. (photo 1975)

Fig. 62. SCARRITT BUILDING, 818 Grand. Built in 1906, Root & Siemens architects. (photo 1973)

Fig. 63. Detail of ornament in rear lobby of SCARRITT BUILDING. (photo 1973)

Fig. 64. GUMBEL BUILDING, 801 Walnut. Built in 1903-04, John W. McKecknie architect. (photo 1973)

Fig. 65. BOLEY CLOTHING COMPANY BUILDING, 1124-1130 Walnut. Built in 1908-09, Louis S. Curtiss architect. (photo 1973)

61

probably the most striking example. At long last a number of high-rise office buildings, using modern structural techniques, were erected. One was the R.A. Long Building, now the United Missouri Bank, of 1906 by Howe, Hoit & Cutler, which was the successor firm to Van Brunt & Howe (Fig. 61). Another major addition in 1906 was the Scarritt Building, one block to the north. It provides us with a fine example of Sullivanesque ornament (Figs. 62 and 63). The architects were Root & Siemens. Walter C. Root was John Wellborn Root's brother, and he remained in Kansas City after arriving here to supervise the latter's work. The Scarritt Building stands as a dramatic contrast to the Renaissance detailing of the Long Building. Another 1906 high-rise office building is the Commerce Bank, by the Chicago architect, Jarvis Hunt. It, like the Long Building, was conservative in its ornament, and it can be seen one block to the rear of the Long Building

in Figure 61. These buildings are generally considered to be the first examples in Kansas City of skyscraper-type construction conceived for buildings of more than ten or twelve stories.

Two smaller structures which were built in the vicinity of the high-rise triad are noted for incorporating structural innovations that were remarkably advanced for their time. One is the Gumbel Building of 1903-04, by John W. McKecknie (Fig. 64). It is a very early example of the large-scale use of structural members made of reinforced concrete. While the ornament of the terra cotta cladding is rather different from that devised by Louis Sullivan, its placement and the overall design of the facades is reminiscent of some of Sullivan's work. The other innovative structure is the Boley Building of 1908-09, which was designed by Louis S. Curtiss (Fig. 65). The extensive areas of glass on the latter's facades are carried on

Fig. 66. FAXON, HORTON, GALLAGHER DRUG COMPANY, 720 Broadway. Built in 1903, Charles A. Smith with Frank S. Rea architects. (photo 1974)

62

floor slabs which are cantilevered past the supporting columns. Thus, we have a very early example of the curtain wall on a large-scale building.

Curtiss, who was involved in the engineering of the caissons for the city hall building, was noted for both his technical know-how and his design work, although, like other architects, he also prepared conservative designs. Despite the importance of his work, he remains a somewhat enigmatic figure, even though he had a comparatively long career in the city. Little is really known about this interesting architect, and the sources of his training are not positively known. Apparently he did go to the Ecole des Beaux-Arts in Paris for interludes of study after coming to Kansas City. What stimuli acted on Curtiss or McKecknie, to help them break with conservative structural techniques and the use of historic ornament at least occasionally, we do not know. Suffice it to say that they did so, and they received support from Kansas City clients during the first decade of this century.

In the wholesale and manufacturing district near Broadway and Eighth which had access to the railroads that skirted the area along the nearby riverfront, additional buildings were erected, such as the one in 1903 for the Faxon, Horton, Gallagher Drug Company (Fig. 66). It was designed by Charles A. Smith in conjunction with Frank S. Rea. Later in 1910, Smith would join with Rea and Walter U. Lovitt and the firm would be responsible for quite a few large buildings in the city before it dissolved in 1922, when Smith became a specialist in school buildings. The drug company building,

Fig. 67. FIRST NATIONAL BANK, northeast corner, Tenth and Baltimore. Built in 1904-06, Wilder & Wight architects. (photo 1976)

with its massive proportions and cautious design, and others like it, aimed at utility but with some attention to the growing use of Renaissance and Neo-classic details. When contrasted to the work done a decade or two earlier (Fig. 59), the discipline and conservatism of the new style can be seen.

A choice example of this growing use of the Renaissance and Neo-classic is the First National Bank Building (Fig. 67). Designed by Wilder & Wight, who opened their office in the city in 1904, the bank was completed in 1906. Wight's brother joined the firm in 1911, and in 1916 the firm became Wight & Wight. The architects had been associated with the McKim, Mead & White firm, and the two Wight brothers had European training as well. In Kansas City they became major exponents of Neo-classicism, and the First National Bank was an important, early statement in that mode. We will hear of the firm again.

Residential architecture in the 1900s covered the full range of sizes, types and building costs, and the entire spectrum of styles was used or adapted in modified form. Some apartment and row houses were built, but the detached house was preferred, even for the most modest of dwellings. No particular style was favored for residences. The variety used is suggested but not fully represented by three homes built in the Northeast District, an area that still retains much of the character it achieved in the early years of this century. A contributing factor in stylistic variety was the wider use of stone. Local stone, which had been common for foundations, was now also being used for half or full exteriors. A number of houses were made of rough-hewn local stone, with random ashlar or even rubble walls. A picturesque example of such a stone house used in conjunction with reinforced concrete is the Flavel Tiffany Residence (Fig. 68). It was built in 1908-09 and designed as a medieval fantasy by Clifton B. Sloan.

In striking contrast, the formal design and finished stone-work of the Calvert Hunt Residence (Fig. 69) speaks of an awareness of the geometricized phase of the Art Nouveau. The architect was John McKecknie, who also designed the Gumbel Building (Fig. 66) in the same year, 1904. He was not adverse to using historic styles, but clearly he was also interested in trying out new trends. Despite this example,

Fig. 68. DR. FLAVEL J. TIFFANY RESIDENCE, 100 Garfield. Built in 1908-09, Clifton B. Sloan architect. (photo 1972)

and some other tentative uses of the Art Nouveau by other architects, comparatively little was done in this style in Kansas City. What remains is mostly some ornamental windows in stained glass.

But most of the architect-designed residences were adaptations of historic styles that were readily available for study and emulation in the handsomely illustrated folio volumes that well-prepared architects included as part of their office libraries. A number of fine designs were in the Georgian style, reflecting a nationwide interest in the Colonial Revival. Colossal, columned porticos were often featured, along with the use of brick walls and white trim, in wood or limestone. The formality and elegance of the exteriors, such as that found in the Judge Walter A. Powell Residence (Fig. 70) by Herman Stroeh, 1909, is a good example of this style as it was used in Kansas City. The English Tudor was also used. These two styles were favored more and more, and they endured in Kansas City as late as the start of World War II (Figs. 88 and 89). Even after the war the styles remained popular, though

63

64

Fig. 69. CALVERT HUNT RESIDENCE, 3616 Gladstone. Built in 1904, John W. McKecknie architect. (photo 1972)

usually in sadly debased versions.

Solid, well-designed residences, the Tiffany, Hunt and Powell houses were built in one of the older sections of the city. To the south, just beyond the city limits, a young, real estate developer, Jesse Clyde Nichols, was beginning a suburban development near a country club, a development that would eventually prove to be a major influence on the city. His plan to create a "high class district on scientific lines" in an area of 1,000 acres was announced in 1908. The following year, that tract and a great deal more became part of the city.

Developers and business people had contributed in a very direct way to the substantial growth of Kansas City. In 1910 a number of them could say they had witnessed phenomenal changes with the result that a large, modern city had replaced the small frontier town within their lifetime. In the forty-five years since the end of the Civil War, the city had come of age, and now some were envisioning a planned metropolis for the site at the great bend of the Missouri River. Considering the accomplishments of the few decades just past, this new dream did not seem beyond the realm of genuine possibility.

Fig. 70. JUDGE WALTER A. POWELL RESIDENCE, 3510 Gladstone. Built in 1909, Herman J. Stroeh architect. (photo 1973)

The Almost Metropolis

In 1910 the city provided some stark contrasts. The recently completed twelve-story skyscrapers towered over a downtown area that now centered along Tenth and Eleventh Street. "Old Town," around Fifth and Main, more and more isolated from the retail businesses and professional offices, was becoming a somewhat dishevelled "civic center." The new park and boulevard system emphasized the inadequacies of older developments and stimulated new planning.

Down in the West Bottoms, the Union Depot in 1910 was woefully out of date. Soon construction would start on a grand, new station near Main and 23rd Street, far south of the old depot and downtown. And throughout the city, especially in the recently annexed areas, new housing was being built. Also, new and better facilities, ranging from schools and hospitals to retail shops, were being constructed for the host of services and business activities that were expected of a growing, first-class city.

While a new and shinier image for the city met civic-minded ambitions, we must not forget that the city, in fact, desperately needed improvements. New construction was required to accommodate a population that had continued to expand rapidly, increasing by over 150,000 from 248,381 in 1910 to 399,736 in 1930.

In Kansas City, construction activity surged significantly to meet growth, most particularly after the construction-hiatus of World War I. The construction peak, in terms of total dollars and numbers of buildings, was reached in 1925. Thereafter, things slowed down, no doubt a reflection of

some overbuilding, but perhaps also evidence of a tapering off, finally, of the population growth. In any case, we can see the shifting patterns when we examine the construction of housing units in the city, particularly in the form of apartment houses.

As noted earlier, Kansas Citians had demonstrated a clear preference for the detached house, though some row houses and apartment dwellings had been built over the years. This preference may well reflect the taste of residents who came to a "western" city, but it may also mirror some characteristics inherent in the local building industry. It is, of course, extremely difficult to reconstruct the history of speculative real estate development that shaped so much of the city's growth. However, it does seem clear that prior to World War I a good deal of residential construction was the work of builders for whom large buildings would either have been too difficult a project, or too expensive for the resources at hand. As the increase in the city's population accelerated, apartment houses must have seemed more attractive housing options to both the developer and resident. There is no question that larger ones, with more units, were constructed in the early 1920s than ever had been the case in previous years. And under these circumstances, it did not take long to saturate the market for this type of housing.

This surge in the construction of apartment units in the early twenties was not simply a matter of increasing the number of buildings built, for we discover that, in fact, a smaller number of apartment houses were built after World

War I than before. If we compare an eight-year period before World War I, 1910 through 1917, to a comparable period from the next decade, 1920 through 1927, we find that in the post-war period fewer apartment buildings were constructed, while the number of apartment *units* was double that built in the pre-war period. What we have then is a significant increase in the average size of apartment houses, going from the typical six-unit building to an *average* of eighteen to twenty-four units, and with some much larger than that. Even though our figures, gleaned from a report by the City Plan Commission, include remodels and apartment units over stores, the striking growth in the number of units built indicates a significant change in the building policy of some developers or the influx of a new type of developer. For the first time in the city one could see a sizable number of large apartment buildings or apartment hotels, often clustered in certain neighborhoods. Some developers and architects even specialized in this type of work. The McCanles Building Company, for example, erected quite a few apartment

Fig. 72. JAMES RUSSELL LOWELL APARTMENTS, 722 Ward Parkway. One of a group of apartment buildings built 1927-29, Nelle E. Peters architect. (photo 1978)

67

Fig. 71. ALAMEDA VISTA APARTMENTS, AND GRANDVIEW APARTMENTS, 4527-31 and 4535 Main Street. Erected 1924-25; demolished 1978. (photo 1977)

houses, including the trio once located at 4527 to 4535 Main Street (Fig. 71). Built in 1924-25, the group which we'll call the Alameda Vista after the name given to two of them, is somewhat transitional in character. They are not high-rise, and they use the multi-deck veranda that had been popular in the city for many years. There is also a repetition of building design, another common feature that sometimes occurred for the length of an entire city block. However, the buildings had eight apartments per floor, for a total of thirty-two units each, and this is clearly in keeping with post-war trends.

Another developer of apartments was the Phillips Building Company. They made extensive use of one architect, Mrs. Nelle E. Peters. In their work together, one can see how the developer could and did influence the appearance of buildings. Some of the work they did together was, to put it quite frankly, rather pedestrian. However, she could and did produce some sensitive designs. Mrs. Peters had a very large

Fig. 73. LUZIER COSMETICS COMPANY BUILDING, 3216 Gillham Plaza. Designed in 1928, Nelle E. Peters architect. (photo 1977)

68

where she began as a draughtsman and remained unregulated in Missouri and Kansas until 1941 and 1949 respectively. While this situation allowed the ill-trained and unqualified to set up in practice, it also bypassed the artificial barriers that otherwise kept women out of many professions. Kansas City has had comparatively few women architects in independent practice in its history. It is noteworthy that of these, Nelle Peters was without question the one who had the most extensive production, one which, in fact, ranked her high among the city's architects in the 1920s.

Many of the 1920s apartment buildings were concentrated in a relatively few locations, such as the immediate vicinity

practice in the 1920s. Her career as an independent architect began in the city in 1909. Except for a few, brief interludes, she continued in practice until 1965. She specialized in apartments and hotels. Typical of her better work in the genre is her group of apartments that Phillips built at Jefferson, Roanoke and Ward Parkway in 1927-29, which he named for literary figures. Representative of these, and of what we might call the uncolonnaded high-rise apartment, is the James Russell Lowell at 722 Ward Parkway (Fig. 72). This too, has eight apartments per floor with a total of sixty-four units in the structure.

Nelle Peters also did other types of buildings, one of which is the laboratory structure for the Luzier Cosmetics Company which she designed in 1928. The facade of the otherwise plain building at 3216 Gillham Plaza is one of her most effective designs (Fig. 73). Nelle Peters' success in a male-dominated profession was derived from her ability to deliver results. But she was given a chance to learn and to compete by the fact that the profession had been unregulated in Iowa

Fig. 74. THE NEWBERN APARTMENT HOTEL, 525 E. Armour. Built in 1921 and 1925, Ernest Brostrom architect. (photo 1972)

Fig. 75. Entrance of THE NEWBERN, 525 E. Armour. (photo 1972)

of the Country Club Plaza, as in the case of the James Russell Lowell and the Alameda Vista Apartments, or along Armour Boulevard on which The Newbern, by Ernest Brostrom, is located (Figs. 74 and 75). The Newbern was built in 1921 as two separate structures. In 1925 Brostrom added the shared entrance and lobby at 525 E. Armour. The architect's admiration for Louis Sullivan and especially Frank Lloyd Wright is clearly evident. The elaborate terra cotta ornament, as well as the meticulously detailed ironwork and leaded glass of the lamps flanking the entrance, show Brostrom's dependence on those master designers. They demonstrate his originality as well.

70

The Newbern and the James Russell Lowell are characteristic of the larger, taller apartment building and apartment hotel that became common after 1920. They form an interesting contrast to the Alameda Vista Apartments. With the increase in height, the multi-deck veranda, that once characteristic and attractive contribution to Kansas City apartment design, was no longer feasible. It was, of course, a design device adapted to meet the hot, humid summers that affect the region, and its local prototype can be traced to the exterior galleries found on ante-bellum houses in the city. The multi-deck veranda for apartment buildings was a logical development of the gallery and of the later, two-story porch found on many of the larger residences. It is difficult to ascertain when colossal Classic columns, as in the Alameda Vista, were first used. One can surmise that the World Fairs, in Chicago in 1893 and St. Louis in 1904, were important influences, as was probably the Colonial Revival movement that occurred at that same time. Correctly detailed and proportioned columns were definitely used for apartment houses in Kansas City in the very early years of the twentieth century, and they were still popular in the mid-1920s. As in the case of the Alameda Vista Apartments, Classic detailing rarely extended beyond the columns which were often placed on pier-stilts to gain the necessary height. This often led to some rather individual solutions to the design of the veranda. One can also find verandas that display rather unusual column or pier designs.

With increases in building height, some alternatives were needed if some sort of individualized porch-type space was to be provided for the tenants. Several options were used in the city, including the roof deck. Ground-level terraces, sometimes sheltered, were another solution. And then there were small porches which were integrated within the facade design, as was originally the case with the James Russell Lowell. Their placement was important, for there was an attempt to provide a maximum of cross ventilation, and on a building with several units per floor, this provided a real challenge to the architect. Porches such as these were often located at a building corner and in projecting bays, and at times the latter became important design features. In recent years, with the wide use of air conditioning, these porches are often glazed and even remodeled into another, regular residential space, a practice that has been widely used on single-family dwellings as well.

Construction of apartment housing was matched in the early 1920s by a similar boom in single-family residences. Using the same periods as before, 1910-1917 and 1920-1927, a comparison shows a 52% increase in the number of residences completed in the post-war period over that of the pre-war. And, analogous to the case of apartment units, there was a noticeable slowdown in construction after the peak, in this case in 1926. As might be expected, a dramatic decline in the construction of both apartments and detached houses occurred after 1929. It is interesting to observe that while the onset of the Great Depression profoundly affected the construction of residential units, it really accelerated a decline that had, in fact, begun several years before the crash of the stock market, probably in response to a slowdown in population growth. Residential construction is, of course, very closely linked to growth in population as well as the economic well-being of the community. It is difficult to isolate the effect of one influence from the other. Business construction, on the other hand, seems less dependent on increases in a city's population. This was certainly the case in Kansas City.

When we turn to the construction of business buildings, which includes office buildings, we see that here, too, there was a significant increase in the number of buildings built in the immediate post-war period. Then after a 1925-26 peak there is a decline. So far the parallel with residential construction holds, but there is one significant difference. While there is a danger in using dollar comparisons, given the fluctuations in wages and prices, we note that despite the decline in the number of business buildings constructed, dollar expenditures remained quite high into the late 1920s. This is quite a contrast to housing where both the numbers of buildings and the dollars spent declined.

If we narrow our focus on the construction of business buildings and compare 1923-26 with 1927-30, we find that though there was a 61% decline in the number of new business buildings in the second period, there was only a 16% decline in their total cost. This anomaly is not simply an indication of inflated prices. Rather, the figures indicate that in Kansas City in the late twenties, there was a commitment to the construction of some very large business buildings, among which were some genuinely tall office buildings. So as the decade ended, Kansas City was gaining for the first time the status symbol of a high-rise skyline, ranging from twenty to thirty stories, with one, the Kansas City Power and Light, topping out at 479 feet (Fig. 105). Conceived or started in the late twenties, most of these towers were finished in the early thirties, and they all are expressive of the growth-is-progress concept that dominated the period, 1910-1930. However, chronologically and stylistically, they are separated from that period. Most were constructed after the stock market crash, and their architects rejected the use of historic eclecticism. It is for these reasons that they should and will be considered with other buildings more obviously integral to the period 1930-1950.

The growth of the population and the increased number and size of buildings were not the only changes in the 1910-1930 period. There also were changes in people's life styles and in their work patterns. Manufacturing and warehousing increased and were becoming more dispersed in the city. Trolley cars had replaced cable cars, and service was being extended to the outlying areas. The 1887 authorization for a second Kansas City bridge over the Missouri River was finally implemented, and the ASB Bridge was completed in 1911 by the Armour, Swift and Burlington interests. This was the same industrial-railroad group that established, in 1912, North Kansas City across the river, creating a separate and largely industrial municipality outside of Kansas City's control.

Within the city, industry was moving into the lower valley of the Blue River, taking advantage of both the water and the rail lines that followed the stream. The construction of the new Union Station began to affect land use south of Nineteenth Street in the midtown area, shifting more of it to uses dependent upon rail transport.

With extensive construction of all sorts underway, it became apparent to city leaders that some controls were needed if the changes were to be generally beneficial. What was sought was the creation of an orderly metropolis, not an unplanned, helter-skelter conglomeration of urban odds and ends. The city had had the positive experience of seeing what a Board of Park Commissioners, organized in 1893, could do, and this was a model that was worth developing. The park board's scope, however, was restricted to the beautification of the city by the creation of parks and boulevards. Thus, a commission with a larger responsibility and more pervasive authority was needed for the task of guiding the total physical development of the city. In 1919 the City Plan Commission was authorized, and early in 1920 the first City Planning Commission was named. The following year the State Zoning Enabling Act was passed by the legislature, and the commission turned to the task of preparing a zoning plan. A report on a tentative zone-plan for the city was published late in 1922, and a final draft was passed in June of 1923. All things considered it was a rapid pace, and for the first time in the city there were effective controls on the use to which ground could be put, the height of buildings, and the area of a lot that could be occupied by a building. Related to that, and from the very beginning, the City Plan Commission also concerned itself with recommendations affecting streets and viaducts. As the 1922 report stated, the regulations were to be "part of a city-wide plan to control the character and extent of the city's growth and are [to be] established in accordance with some definite plan of city development."

71

A factor that had to be part of the planning was the growing use of the private automobile. As early as 1913 a decline in mass transit passengers, on a per capita basis, was noted, presumably a reflection of increased automobile ownership. By 1924, a comprehensive traffic count sponsored by the Engineer's Club confirmed the rise of automobile use, and the first traffic control signals were installed in the more heavily traveled portion of the city. Another indication of the growing impact of the automobile on the city was the nature of the developments sponsored by the J. C. Nichols Company.

As we noted earlier, the realtor and developer, Jesse Clyde Nichols, had announced in 1908 his plan for what we now call the Country Club District. Three years earlier, he had started his first subdivision in the then suburban area south of Brush Creek. By 1907 he expanded the scope of his operation, setting the stage for what proved to be one of the most important developments in greater Kansas City, a project which would prove to be influential throughout the nation. The 1908 announcement in the *Kansas City Star*,

April 28, is worth quoting at length, since it states clearly that planning and rigorous controls would be central to the orderly development of the large area between Holmes and State Line, and 51st and 59th Streets. This same concept would later be extended to other developments in the southwestern part of the city and across the state line, into Johnson County.

A general plan has been adopted by which boulevards, winding roads, stone walls, rustic bridges and circular drives, shelter houses, systematic planting of trees and shrubs, the creation of private parks, the treatment of running streams, work out into a harmonious whole. The old method of laying out in squares regardless of topography is abandoned and the property is so divided as to permit intelligent treatment of hillside or lowland, thus escaping any ugly unsightly cuts or fills.

By 1917 the Country Club District had expanded south to 65th, north across Brush Creek and across the state line to the west. Within this large area, there were in fact some rectangular blocks, but where the terrain suggested curving

Fig. 76. CRESTWOOD SHOPS, 301-337 E. 55th. Built in 1922, Edward W. Tanner architect. (photo 1977)

72

streets and irregularly shaped lots, this was done.

The initial concept had intended to restrict the district to single family residences, with "flats, apartment houses, family hotels, factories and business establishments of any kind" barred. As it would turn out, the J. C. Nichols Company quite early did introduce controlled neighborhood shopping developments to provide services to the residents. The first of these was already in place before the 1908 announcement. This was the small one-story row of shops on the north side of 51st Street, between Brookside and Oak, which were built in 1907. Called "neighborhood shops on the English village plan," they were deliberately modest in scale and fronted by a pillared portico. Rebuilt in 1951, they are now an inconspicuous feature south of the Twin Oaks Apartments. Not too many years later, in 1919, the first unit of a large complex of shops was built at 63rd and Brookside.

Edward Tanner, an architect who was affiliated with the Nichols Company, was responsible for the design of many Nichols-built structures, including the Crestwood Shops on 55th, between Oak and Brookside, which were constructed in 1922 (Fig. 76). Other small "English village shops" were added elsewhere in the district, and some still continue to provide service as originally conceived, though others have been modified in character over recent years. In all cases they were initially designed with a concern that they be compatible with the residential areas they served. They were certainly far different from the conventional retail centers that just simply grew in the city. While convenience for pedestrians and accessibility to public transit routes were factors in their placement and organization, they were situated to serve also the automobile. In this respect they recognized that convenient, free parking for commercial buildings was a factor of growing importance. The J. C. Nichols Company also made provision for filling stations in their planning, and they set aside suitable areas for schools and churches. The most ambitious non-residential project of the company was the acquisition of nearly sixty acres just north of Brush Creek and west of Mill Creek Parkway, now Nichols Parkway, for the development of a regional shopping district.

The land had been assembled by 1912, in what was largely a neglected, marshy section along 47th Street, south to Brush Creek. The plans to reclaim this area and slowly turn it into a first-class shopping district to serve the outlying and suburban residents depended on the prior development of the residential areas in the Country Club District. Consequently, a comprehensive scheme for the shopping district was not announced until 1922. This bold plan, the result of an extended period of work on the part of a number of people, looked to the future. Therefore, a substantial number of buildings were plotted, and there was provision for ample, free, off-street parking. The plan was given substance in an overall design developed by the architect Edward Buehler Delk. Soon thereafter, the first buildings were under construction, following Delk's concept.

Additions, remodelings, and renovations to the shopping center known as the Country Club Plaza have been virtually continuous over the years of its existence. Consequently a simple chronology and a neat list of designers is not readily derived. Initial buildings were Delk's designs. Later, Edward Tanner and his associates would be responsible for continuing much of the architectural development on the Plaza. Work still goes forward, though in recent years several architectural firms have been used.

The first three shop-office buildings were built or completed in 1923. These were the Mill Creek Building (Fig. 77), the Tower Building (Fig. 78), and the Triangle Building. The first two have not changed too much over the years, though all have undergone modifications, especially the Triangle Building, which was named for the shape of the plot. With Delk's initial Plaza plan, there was a commitment to an eclectic style based on Spanish-Mexican motifs. This was Mr. Nichols' wish, and it was continued through the early developmental years. Perhaps the most characteristic features of the early Plaza style are found in the use of towers and in exterior polychromy. The latter was achieved through painted stucco, decorative tiles, terra cotta ornament, tile roofs, and ornamental ironwork. The towers were rather freely adapted from Spanish and Spanish Colonial prototypes.

The Tower Building (Fig. 78), with its shops on the first floor, offices on the second, a corner tower, and with its tiles,

73

Fig. 77. MILL CREEK BUILDING, Country Club Plaza, 4638 Nichols Parkway. Built in 1923, Edward Buehler Delk architect. (photo 1977)

74

terra cotta, and wrought iron balconies, summarizes quite well the basic style. Shop fronts on Plaza buildings, however, have tended to change over the years. The Mill Creek Building, for example, was once graced with a full spread of shop windows that featured mullions in the form of delicate, spiral colonnettes. Also, this interest in picturesque details was matched by a concern for picturesque silhouettes, hence the buildings were not simple variants of one basic design. As we can see in Figure 77, the Tower and Mill Creek Buildings work well together but they are far from similar in appearance. The one-story shop that occupies the recessed corner, where the two join, is a later addition, replacing a small filling station, one of several initially part of the Plaza.

The Plaza planners from the first recognized Kansas City's growing dependence upon the private automobile by the provision for a garage, filling stations, and the construction of free, off-street parking lots. Initially, only walled, surface lots were used, but in more recent years these have given way to multi-deck lots, and parking on the upper levels of newer

buildings. Today, this conscious catering to automobile-based shoppers is the norm and even demanded, so the initiative taken in the Plaza plan does not appear as innovative as, in fact, it was. When first it was implemented, a sizable portion of the population was still without automobiles, and convenient pedestrian or public transit access to downtown or the neighborhood retail center was important.

For the growing population that ringed the Country Club Plaza, the latter perforce served as a neighborhood business district, though one more elegantly conceived and far better planned than the typical conglomerate of shops found at a major intersection. The Plaza was never intended to be simply a group of neighborhood shops and services. But the fact that it was so used by the growing number of apartment dwellers that lived in the immediate vicinity of the Plaza contributed to its initial success through the provision of a density of Plaza-users that single-family dwellings alone would not create. And over the succeeding years, the interdependence of the Plaza and nearby apartment buildings has encouraged the growth of both, until the Plaza area now has one of the highest concentrations of apartment dwellers anywhere in the city. Many are still without automobiles and dependent on the Plaza for their shopping needs.

Recent changes in the Plaza that are aimed to serve better the growing number of hotel-based visitors and automobile-based customers have created some distress among long-time residents, as accustomed services are reduced, modified, or terminated. The Plaza of the 1970s is not the Plaza that was formed in the 1920s. Yet the two are linked and in many ways the Nichols/Delk conception anticipated much of what exists today.

Elsewhere in the city, cinemas, schools, hospitals, commercial and industrial buildings, as well as apartment houses and individual residences were constructed. These helped change the appearance of Kansas City in the years immediately before and after World War I. The quintessential symbol of this change is the Union Station (Fig. 79). It still

Fig. 78. TOWER BUILDING, Country Club Plaza, 114 W. 47th. Built in 1923, Edward Buehler Delk architect. (photo 1977)

stands as evidence of that period's almost unrestrained optimism about the future of the city. It also serves to remind us of the extensive growth that was then occurring in the city, particularly in the recently annexed areas to the south. The impressive bulk of the head house dwarfed the railroad trains as well as the passengers. Its inspiration was quite obviously rooted in Imperial Rome. The colossal scale of the colonnaded arcade of the facade was carried into the interior, where the lofty concourse-lobby, which once stood empty of all but an austere, semicircular ticket office, is still an awesome space, despite the clutter of obtrusive additions (Fig. 80). To the rear of this gigantic interior, an enormous waiting room stretched out, bridging over the tracks and the two-hundred daily trains that once served the city (Fig. 81).

As mentioned earlier, the site of the old Union Depot in the West Bottoms could not be readily expanded to meet the needs generated by city growth. Given its vulnerability to flooding, it was an undesirable location for a new station. However, any new location had to acknowledge the realities of existing right-of-ways and provide for an easy linkage with the established traffic flow and support facilities.

Though several alternate sites were being touted by their supporters, the final choice made in 1906 was clearly the superior in all respects except one: that was its considerable distance from the central business district. The decision to locate the new station in a valley that cut through the bluffs east of the Kansas River, at about 25th Street, seems today to be self evident. The valley, which angled toward the east-northeast (Fig. 27), was used by the Kansas City Belt Railway. Thus feasibility for railroad use was established. At the station site, indicated on Figure 28 by an inverted "T" north of Union Cemetery, at what is now 23rd and Main, the area to the north is fairly level. But to the south there is a rather precipitious rise in the terrain. This configuration encouraged the design of a multi-level station, but it also required that the passenger entrance face south if there was to be street-level access to the lobby and waiting room. This put the entrance on the side opposite of downtown, seemingly turning the station away from the center of town. The through tracks went under the waiting room along the flat,

75

76

Fig. 79. UNION STATION, northwest corner of Pershing and Main. Completed in 1914, Jarvis Hunt (Chicago) architect. (photo 1973)

Fig. 80. GRAND LOBBY AND CONCOURSE, Union Station.
(photo 1978)

and thus below the level of the street facing the entrance. Viaducts on either side of the station permitted the north-south streets to bridge the tracks. All in all it was a most workable arrangement.

The station was built by a consortium of trunk railroads who formed the Kansas City Terminal Railway Company. They selected Jarvis Hunt of Chicago as the architect, and he succeeded in persuading the directors to build a much grander station than they had first envisioned. The result was the third largest passenger station in the United States, exceeded in size only by New York's two giants, the Pennsylvania and the Grand Central Stations.

Hunt's design solution, while workable, was not especially innovative. There were precedents for various aspects, whether the colossal orders of the arcaded facade of the head house or the use of a bridge-like waiting room over the through tracks. However, Hunt was remarkably successful in creating an effective separation of functions, such as isolating arriving passengers from those waiting to board, or in

providing extensive space for baggage, parcel and mail facilities without encroaching on passenger needs. These, along with all of the necessary service components such as restaurants and offices, were encompassed in a monumentally proportioned building with soaring interior spaces, grand vista, and rich detailing. The station was built for a metropolis of a million or more residents, when, in fact, the city had less than three hundred thousand. Even so, it was also designed to be readily expanded, by extending the waiting room and adding gates, platforms and tracks. While the 1910 drawings show a few refinements which were omitted, such as a fountain at the base of the central facade-arch, the station was built substantially as designed. It opened for public use in November 1914.

The impact of the station on the surrounding midtown area was, of course, considerable. Some envisioned a new civic center for the crest of the hill immediately to the south, where the Liberty Memorial now stands (Fig. 90). However, the station had not been the first improvement in the area. By 1904, Penn Valley Park to the southwest of the station was virtually complete. To the east, on the crest of a hill in another park, the city's new General Hospital was completed in 1908. Both parks can be identified in the map of Figure 28. New roadways through the hilly terrain south of the station were needed, and the creation in 1911 of the McGee Street

77

Fig. 81. UNION STATION from the west. (photo 1973)

Fig. 82. FIRESTONE BUILDING, 2001 Grand. Designed in 1915, Smith, Rea & Lovitt architects. (photo 1974)

Still occupied by its initial owner, the austere exterior of the Firestone Building is quietly animated by the slight variations in the widths between the white clad piers and between the mullions. Ornament, of restrained Gothic-inspired motifs, is minimal and reads more as texture than individualized detail. The structure is fully revealed, even to the clear expression on the facade of the elevator shaft. The concern for proportions can be noted in the way the spandrels are divided. All in all, it is a most interesting example of how a basically conservative design can be also expressive of quite contemporary esthetic developments.

Fig. 83. KANSAS CITY CLUB, 1228 Baltimore. Designed in 1918, Smith, Rea & Lovitt architects. (photo 1977)

78

Trafficway, from 22nd to 31st Streets, was an important improvement.

The following year, the Main Street cut was made through the hill to the south of the station, a hill which rose some one hundred feet above the level of the street fronting the station. New manufacturing and warehousing buildings were constructed or planned for the area north of the railroad's right-of-way. An interesting example, both because of its elegant proportions and virtually unchanged exterior, is the Firestone Building (1915) by Smith, Rea & Lovitt (Fig. 82).

Fig. 84. GRAND AVENUE TEMPLE Office Building, 903 Grand. Designed in 1910, John W. McKecknie architect. (photo 1975)

Fig. 85. STINE AND McCLURE UNDERTAKING COMPANY, 924-26 Oak (now Siegrist Engraving Company). Built in 1912, John W. McKecknie architect. (photo 1972)

The same firm, which disbanded in 1922, designed a number of other commercial and office buildings before and after the war. Most were carefully detailed and conservative in design. The high-rise Kansas City Club Building (Fig. 83) at Thirteenth and Baltimore, is perhaps more representative of their work than is the Firestone Building. Designed in 1918, the Club's restrained use of late English Gothic styling, executed in brick and glazed terra cotta, suited very well Kansas City's generally conservative taste. This conservatism acted as a restraint on even the most esthetically aware architects, such as John McKecknie. We saw him as a structural and design leader as early as 1904 (Figs. 64 and 69). By 1910 he was also doing academically eclectic works more typical of the period, such as the Grand Avenue Temple

Fig. 86. CORRIGAN-SUTHERLAND RESIDENCE, 1200 W. 55th, from the southeast. Built in 1913, Louis S. Curtiss architect. (photo 1972)

Fig. 87. CORRIGAN-SUTHERLAND RESIDENCE from the south. (photo 1972)

dressed limestone exterior with its disciplined floral ornament seems far removed from the work of Wright. Nevertheless, there is a kinship with the Prairie School Master in the wide, projecting eaves, the ribbon windows, and in the geometry of interlocking shapes. Located on the northwest corner of 55th and Ward Parkway, the Corrigan-Sutherland House is an especially striking example of Louis Curtiss' work, and the occasional exploration of modernism that did occur, if somewhat tentatively, in Kansas City.

More typical of architect-designed houses in the period 1910 to 1930 are those that were based on the Tudor or Georgian styles. The residence designed by Elmer Boillot in 1927, which is at 1234 Huntington (Fig. 88), is representative of the Tudor influence, while the house at 5367 Cherry, c. 1925, illustrates the Georgian (Fig. 89). It should be noted that both are typically free adaptations rather than slavish imitations. The Georgian style, with its formal qualities, and the Tudor, with its picturesque details and asymmetry, could both be easily escalated in scale and elaborateness, and both were readily adaptable to institutional use. This extensive

81

Office Building, at Ninth Street (Fig. 84). In 1912 he designed the Stine and McClure Undertakers Company Building (now Siegrist Engraving), at 924-26 Oak, in the Egyptian style (Fig. 85). These four McKecknie designs tell us a great deal about both the architecture of the early years of the twentieth century and the architect, and he can be taken as representative of the better designers of his generation. Clearly the architects were influenced by their clients, and a well prepared architect was expected to serve the needs and tastes of others, regardless of what he might personally favor. To do otherwise could easily sink a career.

In residential architecture, there were some cautious investigations of the Prairie School Style associated with Frank Lloyd Wright and his followers, but none was what we could call a textbook example. On the other hand, Louis S. Curtiss, who had produced some innovative work (e.g. the Boley Building, Fig. 65), did explore a variety of design options while still doing some rather conventional work. One of his most ambitious, and certainly one of the most successful residential designs, is the Corrigan-Sutherland House of 1913 (Figs. 86 and 87). Situated on a spacious lot in the Sunset Hill section of the Country Club District, the

Fig. 88. RESIDENCE, 1234 Huntington. Built in 1927, Elmer Boillot architect. (photo 1978)

Fig. 89. RESIDENCE, 5367 Cherry. Built c. 1925. (photo 1978)

82

use of these historic styles was partly an expression of the innate preferences for familiar images, something that historic eclecticism furnished. One suspects it was also a response to the search for symbols of metropolitan maturity such as longer established cities could boast. If a metropolis were, in fact, to take form at the great bend of the Missouri River, and if it were to be convincingly that, tangible symbols were needed to reflect that status. So with the renewed construction after the hiatus of World War I, historic eclecticism served the needs of Kansas Citians, and despite the advances that had taken place in architectural design, taste was channeled primarily toward predictable forms.

The enactment of zoning and planning controls had added to the certainty that civic goals would be reached. Contributing to these ends there were other governmental changes, such as the approval in 1925 of a new city charter. This one introduced the city manager form of government which aimed at more efficient, businesslike management of city affairs. As it would turn out, however, it also proved to be susceptible to corruption. In short order, with the compliance of a self-serving group on the City Council, the city manager's office ceased to be accountable for its actions, and by the early 1930s, mismanagement of city affairs became rampant. Yet, initially the new charter was seen as central to the effort to create a vehicle to ensure a bright future for the growing city.

Characteristic of this vision was the drive to fund a gigantic monument to the dead of World War I. While symbolically a clear link to the past, Liberty Memorial (Fig. 90) was also evidence of progress appropriate to the new image of the city. The public became thoroughly involved in the discussion over what would be a suitable memorial, and it was not surprising that a grand monument, such as could be found in major cities, rather than a utilitarian memorial, was chosen. The selection of the site on the crest of the hill south of the Union Station was also in keeping with the spirit if not the scope of earlier plans for a civic center at that location. Fund raising involved all segments of the population, and the design was selected through a national competition. The original expectations held for both the memorial and the site were not fully realized, and what eventuated required some years' time. But when the design of H. Van Buren Magonigle was dedicated in 1926, there was no doubt that here was a fitting companion to Jarvis Hunt's Union Station. Both were suitable civic images for the city then abuilding. Both are also structures in the best tradition of early twentieth century, Beaux-Arts monumentalism. That both were also the work of non-Kansas City architects (Magonigle was from New York) was more a matter of individual circumstances than any lasting reflection on the talent of the designers in Kansas City.

Local architects had sought the commissions for both the Union Station and the war memorial. As we review the history of architectural patronage in the city, more often than one might have expected, local architects were, in fact, used by Kansas City clients. The exceptions are often easily explained, as when the client was not a native of Kansas City, as was the case of the Federal Reserve Bank (Fig. 91) by Graham, Anderson, Probst & White of Chicago (1919). In some cases the specialized experience of architects could be a

Fig. 90. LIBERTY MEMORIAL, southwest corner Pershing and Main, view from the north. Built 1923-36, H. VanBuren Magonigle (New York) architect. (photo 1973)

84

Fig. 91. FEDERAL RESERVE BANK, 923-33 Grand. Built in 1919, Graham, Anderson, Probst & White (Chicago) architects. (photo 1975)

appropriate to its function, another contribution of historic eclecticism appreciated in that period.

Specialization was becoming important in architecture. While Kansas City had its own experts in the design of motion picture theatres, the Boller Brothers, it was understandable that the Loew's Theatre chain, with their national interests, would choose a New York expert, Thomas W. Lamb, as the principal architect while also retaining the Boller Brother's firm. Their task was to create the grandest of the movie palaces built in Kansas City, and one of the most impressive anywhere. This was the Midland Theatre on Main Street at Thirteenth, built in 1927 (Fig. 92).

While the use of non-local architects might seem to have created disadvantages for Kansas City architects, it must be remembered that they, in turn, designed buildings erected outside of the city, a situation applicable to the Boller Brothers. Some architects had active Kansas practices in addition to their Missouri work. Indeed, there is some evidence that Kansas City served as a regional resource in the provision of architectural services.

It is hard to decide if local architects alone could have generated the design of the Midland Theatre, which had an attached office building facing on Baltimore. Probably some could have. The restraint of the exterior design is tempered by a broken pediment and niche that mark the location of the theatre's entrance. This anticipates the interior which tosses restraint aside in a sumptuous display of rich ornament inspired by opulent Baroque examples. In the finest tradition of the "movie palace," it was filled with works of art, great mirrors and glittering chandeliers (Fig. 93). The carved wood, the ornamented plasterwork, and the polychromy created a wonderland that in many ways is more impressive today than when it was built. In Kansas City it was not the only theatre to emulate the features of a princely palace, or to provide a setting that allowed one's sense of fantasy to play. But with 4,000 seats, it was the largest and the most impressive. It was, in a manner of speaking, a theatre-variant of the Union Station in its bigness and in its symbolic value to the aspiring city.

The movie palace, with its exuberant use of rich ornament

factor, and this too was relevant in the matter of the Federal Reserve. At the equivalent of twenty stories, the Federal Reserve Bank was for its day the tallest building in the city. And Graham, Anderson, Probst & White, as the successor to the D. H. Burnham Company, had made its mark as designers of tall buildings. The staid, cut-stone Neo-classicism of the Federal Reserve's design can be considered as symbolically

Fig. 92. MIDLAND THEATRE and Office Building, 1228-34 Main; 1221 Baltimore. Built in 1926-27, Thomas W. Lamb (New York) and Boller Brothers architects. (photo 1976)

and period furnishings, was peculiarly a product of the twenties, though one can find stylistic precedents in earlier opera houses and other legitimate theatres. On the other hand, the development of airports presented new architectural problems for which precedents were lacking. The year the Midland opened (1927), a municipal airport for Kansas City was dedicated.

Located on the flood plain within the Missouri River bend, it was at first little more than a dirt field behind its dikes. Two years later, improvements were made which included construction of a small passenger terminal. That modest structure, of course, gave no hint of the challenge that air travel would provide to the railroads. And the monumental Union Station, virtually in mint condition in 1929, was obviously the appropriate gateway to the maturing, twentieth century city. Some forty years later, not only had the initial air terminal been enlarged and then replaced, a new airport with three enormous terminal buildings would be moving toward completion and the Union Station's future would be in question.

Somewhat more durable needs were being met by large-scale industrial and warehouse buildings, such as the Montgomery Ward Building of 1913 and 1918 (Fig. 94). Of reinforced concrete, this large mail order store at Belmont and St. John, was designed by McKecknie & Trask. Basically a utilitarian design, its visual strength comes primarily from the repetition of structural members along the lengthy facades. The limited ornament is an interesting amalgam of traditional and modern forms. But more times than not, structure was hidden behind conventional exteriors with readily recognized ornament.

Perhaps there was a concern that new directions in architecture might prove inadequate, and design failures would retard Kansas City's growth, a growth that would hopefully make it a competitive, commercial center of the Middle West. Extensive manufacturing activities were added to the transportation, agribusiness, and jobbing base, and extensive new areas for housing were opened up. One could see the start of genuinely tall office buildings on the skyline, and there was a clear tendency to follow tried and proven architectural paths. This is particularly evident in the large mansions that were built in the city and nearby suburbs in the 1920s.

As a matter of course the better houses were architect-designed. At times they were extraordinarily impressive in concept, bulk and detailing. Such was the case of the large Tudor manor house which U.S. Epperson built in 1924-27, and which is now part of the University of Missouri-Kansas City campus (Fig. 95). A design of Horace LaPierre, with Epperson's active collaboration, the house was only one of many large mansions built in this period in the southwest section of the city. LaPierre is best known for his residential work from the later years of his career. He is but one of quite a large number of architects who are remembered for their house designs from this period and into the 1930s. Another, Edward Tanner, was a prolific designer of residences in addition to his commercial work, most done during his long association with the J. C. Nichols Company. The same was

85

86

Fig. 93. Detail of inner lobby of MIDLAND THEATRE. (photo 1976)

Fig. 94. MONTGOMERY WARD BUILDING, 6200 St. John. Built in 1913 with addition in 1918, McKecknie & Trask architects. (photo 1978)

true of Edward Buehler Delk, whose work was varied and spread over quite a few years.

A list of individuals and partnerships that were responsible for fine home design in this period would be quite extensive. One, however, merits special attention, for she was one of those very few women architects whose active career extended over a fairly long time span. This is Mary Rockwell Hook. She, like Nelle Peters, had the drive and talent to compete in an unregulated profession that was not very hospitable to women, and she had a successful practice, part of which was in partnership in the late twenties with E.D.M. (Mac) Remington. She concentrated primarily on fine homes for wealthy individuals. Her earliest built design is a small house for herself in 1908. Her best known work in the city is concentrated in the Sunset Hill area. There, in a compound of three houses designed for her family, one can find another house she built for herself (Fig. 96). It dates to 1922, and it is quite typical of her avoidance of identifiable historic styles, while still tending toward the picturesque. She often incorporated fragments from older structures, and she was quite successful in designing houses for rugged, sloping sites, a characteristic of the northern portion of the Sunset Hill area.

On the other hand, the bulk of housing built in this period,

from modest bungalows to some fairly sizable two-story residences, were the work of contractor-builders placing homes on standard lots. Bungalows were very popular in this period with most being rather modest stock designs selected from pattern books. The bungalow proved to be a versatile solution to the need for quick production of small, detached houses. With their variety of porches, flexibility of plan, and options in finish, they had the potential of great individuality in appearance while still allowing use of stock millwork, and construction using a small crew. Bungalows ranged from the extraordinarily simple, and even primitive, to some which were fairly ambitious in finish and treatment. While most were frame structures, sometimes with stucco finish, others were veneered in brick or stone as exemplified by a group on Rockhill Road (Fig. 97).

We know that some architects were associated with real estate developers. It is possible that the more ambitious bungalow, as with the slightly more pretentious, two-story tract house, incorporated modifications designed by archi-

87

Fig. 95. U. S. EPPERSON RESIDENCE, southwest corner of 52nd and Cherry, now EPPERSON HOUSE, University of Missouri-Kansas City. Built 1924-27, Horace LaPierre architect. (photo 1976)

88

Fig. 96. MARY ROCKWELL HOOK RESIDENCE, 4940 Summit. Built in 1922-23, Mary Rockwell Hook architect. (photo 1977)

many aspects of the history of architecture were mined for ornament if not entire facades. In this respect, Kansas City was no different from other parts of the United States. If there were any emphases, English country residences of the 17th and 18th centuries provided the inspiration for detached homes and some duplexes. In commercial buildings, English Gothic ornament was almost as popular as Renaissance and Baroque forms, but there was also a growing interest in Neo-classicism. Churches and schools ranged widely in their designs, with perhaps a slight preference shown for post-Medieval styles.

The growth of Neo-classicism in Kansas City, with some admixture of forms derived from the early Italian Renaissance, was strongly influenced by the firm of Wight & Wight, formerly Wilder & Wight (Fig. 67). A good example of their work from this period and in this vein is the Kansas City Life Building (Fig. 98) of 1923. Wight & Wight's adaptation of the Greek Doric to an office building was quite successful, and it represented the conservative end of quality design. The other end of the spectrum retained ornament, although here it was non-historically derived.

Until the late twenties, the modernists were not too

tects, thereby individualizing what were otherwise stock plans. Whatever the variations, one common feature in the Kansas City area was the elevated sleeping porch found on a great many houses. On the simpler bungalow, this was simply a projection at the rear of the attic. On more sophisticated designs, such as the Rockhill group, it was better integrated into the design. In two-story houses, a sleeping porch was usually incorporated as a side unit, and not infrequently placed in tandem over an open porch, as can be seen on the right in the Georgian style house in Figure 89. What was important, regardless of design, was the provision of a maximum of cross ventilation, from at least three sides through a large number of windows.

Housing, as we have seen, ranged widely in type and quality, and our few examples barely sample the variety. A similarly broad spectrum exists for commercial designs, so it is difficult to sum up all of the architectural characteristics of this twenty-year period in a few words. But some features do stand out. This is the period of historic eclecticism, and

Fig. 97. RESIDENCES, 5700 to 5714 Rockhill Road. Built c. 1926. (photo 1978)

evident. Their ornament tended to consist of flat, rather geometricized designs, sometimes based on floral motifs (Fig. 104). In some cases, for example, The Newbern (Fig. 75), the influence of Frank Lloyd Wright was evident. But regardless of style, a good deal of the ornament used in this period was executed in glazed terra cotta.

Terra cotta for architectural embellishment had been widely used in the city since the late nineteenth century. However, the development of skyscraper-type construction, which originally used tile casings on steel frames for fire-proofing, seemed to stimulate the use of terra cotta for the exteriors in lieu of brick and/or stone. This mold-made cladding material was easily textured, colored, and ornamented. In fact, this treatment helped conceal warping and imperfections in the tiles which more and more were used for entire facades. Given the mass production procedures used in the manufacturing of complete exteriors, the trend toward flatter, more crisply linear, and more mechanically designed ornament was a logical move. Mold-making could then be based on drawings furnished by the architect rather than on the intermediate step of three-dimensional models. As we survey the process, one cannot help but speculate that the rise of the Art Deco style in terra cotta, and in stone, in the late 1920s may have been as much a matter of economy, of time and labor, as of esthetic preference. At least so it appears when we look at the case of Kansas City's architecture.

The ornament on the exterior of the Midland Theatre (Fig. 92) includes a great deal of extraordinarily detailed terra cotta in fairly high relief and in some instances in the round. With its rich, figurative details and sculpturesque character, it represents one extreme in terra cotta ornament used in this period. Related to this bold ornament is the architectonic use of projecting cornices, moldings and the like (Fig. 84). But more typically, the ornament was flatter, used in repetitive patterns, often in bands as in Figures 82 and 83. In most instances, the ornament is neither original in design nor in its placement. We can see the latter (placement) in the case of The Newbern (Figs. 74 and 75). Brostrom's placement of the ornament at the top of piers and around the entrance follows historical precedent, but the ornament itself, especially

Fig. 98. KANSAS CITY LIFE INSURANCE COMPANY BUILDING, 3520 Broadway. Original unit built in 1923, Wight & Wight architects. (photo 1978)

89

around the entrance, was clearly modernist in design.

It is worth comparing The Newbern's entrance with an almost exact contemporary which uses traditional design done in high relief. The entrance of the Acme Cleansing Company Building (Fig. 99), by Archer and Gloyd (1925) is easily traced back to illustrations of Italian Renaissance terra cotta that were published, for exactly this type of use, in the early years of the century. Brostrom's designs are far removed from the fifteenth century, being influenced by Sullivan and Wright. Perhaps it was this inspiration that gave him an independent originality that makes The Newbern's entrance much more than a replica of another's design, as is the case with the Acme's entrance.

At times some of the terra cotta was polychromed, and the facade of the Luzier laboratory (Fig. 73) is representative of how this type of ornament functioned within an overall facade design. Polychromed ornament is found on all sorts of buildings, but perhaps more frequently on smaller structures. This might reflect a conviction that the decorative impact of polychromy would be more readily appreciated if closer to

90

Fig. 99. Entrance for ACME CLEANSING COMPANY BUILDING, 3200 Gillham Road. Designed 1924, Archer & Gloyd architects. (photo 1977)

Fig. 100. SOUTHWESTERN BELL TELEPHONE COMPANY BUILDING, 324 E. Eleventh. First fourteen stories built in 1919, additional fourteen stories built in 1929, Hoit, Price & Barnes architects. (photo 1974)

the viewer, though one can find exceptions. On high-rise structures clad in terra cotta, ornament that was located near the top was more often in bold relief than in colors. At times it was pierced so that there would be strong contrasts of light and shade (Figs. 84 and 83).

An excellent example of such a high-rise was the 1929 facade of the Southwestern Bell Telephone Company Building at Eleventh and McGee (Figs. 100 and 101). The building was built in two stages. The first fourteen stories were erected in 1919, with a second fourteen added in 1929. The architects

Fig. 101. Detail of terra cotta ornament at upper level on the SOUTHWESTERN BELL TELEPHONE COMPANY BUILDING. (photo 1974)

92

Fig. 102. ELEVENOAK BUILDING, formerly SOUTHWESTERN BELL TELEPHONE COMPANY BUILDING. Remodeled 1974-1976. (photo 1978)

in both instances were Hoit, Price & Barnes, a firm that soon became leading practitioners in the city, especially for tall buildings. In both stages the building was given Gothicized detailing, and the stepback parapets of the 1929 addition were particularly impressive examples of bold relief ornament and how it functioned. The past tense has to be used in this case, because while the building still stands its original facade does not. It was veneered and color added in 1974-76. The stucco of marble aggregate and the paint were an attempt by a new owner to modernize the exterior in conjunction with an interior renovation. The resulting appearance (Fig. 102) is a powerful reminder of the sensitively scaled original Hoit, Price & Barnes exterior. Whatever the accumulated problems of the aging cladding, the solution selected represents more than an esthetic choice. It also signals some of the major problems associated with historic preservation. But more on that later.

The two-part construction of the Telephone Building, argued for a continuation of an earlier mode of cladding design. By 1929, however, one can find some interesting alternatives to that style. The Professional Building (Fig. 103), which was designed in 1929, illustrates a different approach to ornament executed in terra cotta. A simple, sixteen-story block by Charles A. Smith and George E. McIntyre, the Professional Building at Eleventh and Grand is sheathed in a buff-textured terra cotta that localized most of the decoration in the upper stories and the entrance (Fig. 104). The flattened, incised design, in which floral patterns have been geometricized, is in the style we now call Art Deco. Rather mechanical in appearance, it was certainly easier to execute than the complex modeling used on the Telephone Building. Whether the architects were motivated by economy or an appreciation of the new styles, or both, is immaterial. The use of accurately detailed, historically-based ornament was beginning to decline at the end of the decade. In time, terra cotta itself would fade away as a major cladding material.

As the 1920s neared an end, while there was still a substantial amount of major office building construction underway, and while residential construction was still quite active, plans were launched to win approval for a major bond

Fig. 103. PROFESSIONAL BUILDING, 1103 Grand. Built in 1929-30, Charles A. Smith and George E. McIntyre architects. (photo 1978)

Fig. 104. Detail of terra cotta ornament over entrance of the PROFESSIONAL BUILDING. (photo 1975)

93

issue to support a variety of public improvements at both the city and county levels. The two-thirds majority needed to win bond approval always made it difficult to secure the passage of any issue. So it was not surprising that most failed to pass in the election of 1928.

Plans were instituted to resubmit the failed bonds to the voters. Before this new proposal was ready for the ballot, the stock market collapsed in 1929, and the economy was so transformed that a far different situation faced the city than it had in 1928. The metropolis that some had envisioned as inevitable at the bend of the Missouri River was now at the very least, postponed. The 1930 census would confirm that the population gains that had become an accepted way of life for the past sixty years were likely over. In fact, by 1930 the population had ceased to grow. The brave symbol of anticipated greatness, the Union Station, would remain forever oversized. The city entered the most difficult period in its history since the harsh years of the Civil War.

The Lean Years

The impact of the economic crisis that would scar the 1930s was masked at first when it came to the architectural scene, for at the turn of the decade there were a number of impressive buildings under construction. Two of these were quite notable for a city that did not have a soaring skyline. These were the Kansas City Power and Light Company Building, and the Fidelity Bank, both designed by the firm of Hoit, Price & Barnes.

The Kansas City Power and Light Building at Fourteenth and Baltimore (Fig. 105), for years the tallest in the state at 479 feet, was completed in 1931. It is still a dominant feature of the city's skyline that since has had a number of tall additions. The building is distinguished by a telescoping, vertical perspective that is emphasized by its square plan and a capping finial. The recessed windows and the angular glass crown of the finial (Fig. 106) are illuminated at night with a cycle of changing colors. The building is sheathed in Indiana limestone. There is carved ornament at key locations on the exterior, most notably at the parapets and on the finial where crisp, clean planes and edges create a bold relief in the Art Deco style, a style repeated in the glasswork. The exterior design is credited to Edwin M. Price of the firm.

It was, for Kansas City, a major step toward modernism, a change particularly evident when we compare the Power and Light with earlier high rises, such as the Federal Reserve Bank that had been completed in 1919 (Fig. 91). The latter is basically a block, with sheer walls rising its entire height. The Power and Light, on the other hand, has several stepbacks that exaggerate the building's verticality, a feature accented also by the use of recessed window spandrels. In contrast, strong horizontals on the Federal Reserve divide the facade into three parts. The Neo-classic detailing further restrains the upward movement that the building actually possesses.

Stepbacks were required on especially tall buildings in Kansas City with the enactment of the zoning ordinance of 1923. This provision was modeled on New York City's law of 1916, which permitted towers of indefinite height after a predetermined set back level, and only if the area of the tower was limited in accordance with a formula keyed to the overall size of the lot. Similar requirements had been enacted in Chicago.

The first building in Kansas City that was required to have set backs was the Southwestern Bell Telephone Building when its height was increased to twenty-eight stories in 1929 (Fig. 100). By then there were ample precedents in other cities to guide the architects. It seems that with the need to continue the earlier commitment to Gothic ornament, there was some influence from the Chicago Tribune Tower, a building which had been erected a few years earlier and which had been extraordinarily well publicized by the international competition that attracted over 200 submissions. The Telephone Building shows a restrained use of stepbacks, with three clustered near the top of the building.

In contrast, Hoit, Price & Barnes used more set backs on the Power and Light. These extend over half the total height, moving back and forth between the lateral facades and the

principal facade on the east. The recessions thereby become much more integral in the dynamics of the building's total exterior organization. The Power and Light is still one of Kansas City's most interesting building silhouettes, and the firm's advancement in the use of set backs and in contemporary ornament in the brief interlude between the Telephone Building's design and that of Power and Light's is quite striking.

If we survey a number of tall buildings, such as the New York Life of 1890 (Figs. 53 and 54), the R. A. Long of 1906 (Fig. 61), the Grand Avenue Temple Office Building of 1910 (Fig. 84), and finally the Federal Reserve and the Telephone Buildings of 1919 and 1929, we see ornament that is historically derived. The notable exceptions in the city prior to the end of the twenties are the Scarritt Building of 1906 (Fig. 62) and The Newbern of 1921/25 (Figs. 74 and 75). The shift in taste toward non-historically derived ornament was coupled with a trend toward flatter, less plastic shapes. This has been discussed in conjunction with the Professional Building (Figs. 103 and 104) which marks the timing of the shift, 1929-30. The Power and Light Building confirms the trend at least for high-rise buildings. The Professional Building's height did not require set backs, and so the ornament was simply a way to provide visual interest as the building terminated against the sky, and to give emphasis to the doorway. Serving a less demanding role than in the Power and Light, the ornament on the Professional Building appears more as texture than sculpture. On the other hand, ornament on the Power and Light is bolder, more simply detailed, and it is used more sculpturally. We should note that this may be partially an architect's preference, but we observe how well it functions at parapet edges to give a transition for set backs. Function here may have dictated form. Certainly this is the case in the ornament which is used to enhance the finial as a focal point in the total composition of the building. Art Deco design was clearly flexible enough to be used in two very different ways on two rather different buildings, and one can understand its

95

Fig. 105. KANSAS CITY POWER AND LIGHT COMPANY BUILDING, 1330 Baltimore. Completed in 1931, Hoit, Price & Barnes architects. (photo 1976)

96

Fig. 106. Detail of upper portion of the tower of the KANSAS CITY POWER AND LIGHT COMPANY BUILDING. View from the east. (photo 1975)

growing attraction for architects.

The architectural firm of Hoit, Price & Barnes received the commission for the Power and Light Building in 1930, and concurrently the firm was selected by the Fidelity Bank and Trust Company to design its new building at Ninth and Walnut. Though not quite as tall as the Power and Light, the Fidelity Bank is more massive. It presents a broad facade (facing Walnut) that makes it a commanding image on the skyline (Figs. 107 and 108). By 1931, the Fidelity Bank was far enough along to win a local AIA design award. This impressive building of thirty-five stories, enormous by Kansas City criteria, has lost some of its visual impact since it was completed in 1932, for there are additional high-rise structures in its vicinity. But for thirty years it anchored one end of the skyline with the Power and Light at the other end.

The bank building terminates in a pair of short towers now joined by a Weather Service radome on a skeletal tower. These towers were a deliberate continuation of a design feature from the bank's previous building which had been on the same site. That first structure had been the 1884 Federal Building (Fig. 41), which the bank occupied in 1902. It was for this reason that the new building also continued the symbolism of having a clock in the north tower, a feature that has since been removed. On the 1932 building, the banking floors were at the lowest levels. These stood as a rectangular mass faced with Indiana limestone occupying the full extent of the lot. The remainder of the building is set back and is clad in brick and terra cotta ornament, the latter in a somewhat Neo-classic style. The Power and Light Building seems the more successfully realized composition, one which is more fully integrated from ground level to the top of the building. One suspects the restraining hand of the patron in the banking structure. Even so, it is a representative statement in office building design of the period, along with the Power and Light and the Telephone Building. Together these structures mark the importance of Hoit, Price & Barnes as architects of

Fig. 107. FIDELITY BANK AND TRUST COMPANY BUILDING, 911 Walnut (later a federal government office building). Completed in 1931, Hoit, Price & Barnes architects. (photo 1978)

Fig. 108. Detail of upper portion of the FIDELITY BANK AND TRUST COMPANY BUILDING. View from the northwest. (photo 1976)

the period between the World Wars.

One characteristic of office buildings at this time is the Beaux-Arts formalism of the symmetrical design of the principal facade. Another characteristic is the way the ornament is used, continuing a tradition where ornament is integral to the overall design concept. The next stage in high-rise design in the city would see the gradual reduction of ornament to the point where very little was used, and that typically would be confined to the entrance areas.

The Bryant Building at Eleventh and Grand, by the Chicago firm of Graham, Anderson, Probst & White (Fig. 109), is a case in point. That firm's earlier tower in Kansas City, the nearby Federal Reserve Building of 1919, was executed in the older tradition of high-rise design, while the Bryant, that was completed in 1931, is clearly committed to the modernism of its day. Like the Power and Light Building, it presents a formally organized facade using set backs and recessed spandrels. A decidedly more vertical emphasis has been created by making many of the spandrels dark. Such ornament as is used is simple and linear, rather than plastic, and it is virtually invisible above the three lower stories which are clad in granite. White glazed brick and terra cotta spandrels in two colors are used for the remainder of the building, which is twenty-six stories high. There is a stripped down quality to the Bryant which originally was floodlighted at night. Along with the vertical dynamics of the facade, it is the most modern of the tall buildings built in the city in this period. One reason for this is that the Bryant's design is an adaptation of Eliel Saarinen's competition design (1922) for the Chicago Tribune Tower, a design that despite its second prize award many felt was the best submitted in that large competition. As far as this writer knows, the Bryant appears to be the only building ever built that emulated the totality of Saarinen's design, though it is hardly a slavish copy. As such it has interest beyond its role in the city's architectural history.

With the construction of these tall buildings, as well as other large commercial structures in the downtown area, the years of 1930 and 1931 proved to have been very active architecturally for the city. This had helped conceal, as we noted before, the deepening economic depression that was soon to become much more evident when virtually all large-scale, privately financed construction ceased after the Fidelity Bank was completed.

Meanwhile, there was also a creeping political corruption in the city's government, a government that was theoretically non-partisan but in fact was intensely partisan and committed to boss rule and a greedy spoils system. In 1931, this government busied itself with plans to submit once again a

Fig. 109. BRYANT BUILDING, 1102 Grand. Built in 1930-31, Graham, Anderson, Probst & White (Chicago) architects. (photo 1973)

98

major bond program to the voters. If approved, the bonds would permit launching an important program of building. So when a campaign was started to seek their passage—which included resubmission of those bonds that failed to pass in 1928—general support was easily gained despite the possibility of shady handling of the funds. As is so often the case, excellent people of unquestionable rectitude either did not see corruption as a problem or managed to rationalize it given the benefits implicit in the program of construction.

The joint city-county effort was labeled the "Ten-Year Plan." Successful passage, which still required a two-thirds majority, was seen by many as a way in which local government could mitigate the damaging effects of the deepening depression. Therefore, it is not surprising that all of the proposals passed with overwhelming majorities in a very large turnout when the election was held in May, 1931. Boss-rule was founded on a deliverable vote, however arrived at, but the issues also seemed to generate genuine popular support. The promise of modern and updated facilities, ranging from a new City Hall and a new County Courthouse, to improvements for parks and for the airport, to still more miles of modern roads was attractive, as was the opening up of many jobs which was implicit in all of these projects. An awareness of the multiplier effect of that money working its way through the local economy undoubtedly also contributed to the passage of all of the proposals.

From our latter-day vantage point, we can see that passage also guaranteed that there would be public facilities to match the buildings recently erected by private sources. So possibly the lure of the Metropolis of the Midlands, which might yet be realized, also contributed to the victory for the bonds.

As things turned out, the federal government also began a major public works program. In addition to new federal buildings, federal funds could be joined to local monies to ensure the completion of local structures that, by and large, turned out to be rather successful buildings. In addition, this infusion of federal money meant that there would also be federal inspectors who were additional watchdogs to protect the public's interest against the agents of local corruption.

Among the buildings sponsored by the city and the county,

three stand out because of their civic importance, their size, and the quality of their design. These are the Municipal Auditorium, the City Hall, and the County Courthouse, Kansas City Division. The need to meet federal criteria, coupled with what we might call an edifice complex on the part of city leaders provided the circumstances that produced two large buildings for the city, both replete with fine materials and excellent workmanship. The County Courthouse also benefited from the watchful eye and the rectitude of Harry S Truman, then the Presiding Judge of Jackson County. Within a three-year span, from late 1935 to late 1937, these three large buildings were dedicated and opened for use.

Had their predecessors really outlived their usefulness? When the City Hall (Fig. 55) had been built in 1890-91, it was desperately needed to serve the growing city, and the County Courthouse of 1892 (Fig. 56), was needed to replace the 1872 structure that had been destroyed by a tornado. Convention Hall, built in 1900, met a need that no other structure then could accommodate. Granted, each had aged, and the city had grown considerably since their construction. But the pressing needs that led to their being built at the end of the nineteenth century were not present when their replacements were first proposed on the bond issue ballot in 1928. In fact, there were arguments that the existing structures were capable, with some renovations, of serving for additional years. Yet, one could point out that the population of the city had increased 200% since 1890.

The area in and around the old public square had aged and deteriorated to the point where it had little semblance to a civic center appropriate to a major city. Convention Hall, the ninety-day wonder rushed to completion after a disastrous fire wrecked its newly built predecessor, meeting a deadline of a national political convention, was clearly limited in its resources. But one negative vote could offset two affirmative ballots, and so the issue of replacement had failed in 1928. Yet three years later the issues carried overwhelmingly. Three additional years of structural age alone could not have made the difference between the outcomes of the two bond submissions. There had to be some other factor.

100

Fig. 111. Detail of lobby, CITY HALL. (photo 1977)

The combined bond propositions, twenty in all, amounted to nearly $48 million. The vision of all of this money entering the economy in a ten-year period, even though borrowed from the future, was clearly more important in 1931 than in 1928. Then, too, there was a symbolic and functional importance to new facilities in a city that had demonstrated great ambitions and which had, along with the rest of the nation, fallen on hard times. However, one suspects that the vision of public works employment coupled with an energetic, machine-turnout of voters, provided the key to success. Yet the appeal of large, modern buildings and a new "uptown civic center" had to have been a contributing factor. When one could actually visit the up-to-date, multi-purpose Mu-

Fig. 110. CITY HALL, 414 E. Twelfth. Completed in 1937, Wight & Wight architects. (photo 1973)

nicipal Auditorium, or see the splendor of the skyscraper City Hall, it would have been hard not to be aware that a major step had been taken in planning the future of the city. These new buildings did, in fact, generate civic pride in much the same way as had the Union Station when it was opened a generation earlier. Grouping the City Hall, the County Courthouse, and a Municipal Courts Building provided a solid nucleus for a true civic center. This was

Fig. 112. JACKSON COUNTY COURTHOUSE (Kansas City Division), 415 E. Twelfth. Completed in 1934, Wight & Wight, Keene & Simpson, and Frederick C. Gunn architects. (photo 1976)

Fig. 113. ORCHESTRA PROMENADE AND LOBBY, MUNICIPAL AUDITORIUM. From Zachman (ed.), *The New Municipal Auditorium* (1936). (SC-UMKC)

Fig. 114. MUNICIPAL AUDITORIUM, Thirteenth to Fourteenth, Wyandotte to Central. Completed in 1935, Hoit, Price & Barnes, with Gentry, Voskamp & Neville architects. (photo 1973)

certainly a tangible sign of civic maturity and of a promise that there would be continued municipal growth. The use of architecture for these purposes is as old as western civilization. Only the types of buildings used to serve this role change. Today, urban America finds its symbols in something other than civic centers, but in the depression of the middle-1930s they served well enough.

Before the end of 1931, the site for the Municipal Auditorium had been assembled and work begun on excavating the square block from Thirteenth to Fourteenth, from Wyandotte to Central. As it turned out, however, four more years would elapse before the auditorium would be fully operational.

The first major government structure constructed in the city in the 1930s was a large Post Office Building at Pershing and Broadway, near the Union Station (Fig. 115). Work had proceeded rapidly on this large facility that was connected by tunnel under Pershing Road to the baggage levels of the railroad station, and it opened in late September, 1933, only seventeen months after the cornerstone had been laid.

While the Post Office was nearing completion, excavation began for the County Courthouse on Twelfth, between Oak and Locust. Less than eighteen months later, in December, 1934, the Courthouse was dedicated (Fig. 112). The Municipal Auditorium (Fig. 114) was the third in sequence of completions, with actual construction starting in 1934. It was dedicated at the end of October, 1935. The fourth major civic structure was the City Hall (Fig. 110), facing the Courthouse across Twelfth Street. It became the official seat of city government twenty-two months after construction started. Its completion in late 1937 opened the way for the demolition of the old City Hall, the adjacent police headquarters and the old market building on Main between Fourth and Fifth, permitting new market facilities to be constructed. The Municipal Courts Building and Police Headquarters, located at the northeast corner of Twelfth and Locust, was built in 1938 (Fig. 117). In that year, demolition of the old Federal Building on Grand, between Eighth and Ninth (Fig. 57) was completed and work began on the new Federal Courts Building and Post Office that was finished in 1939 (Fig. 116).

Fig. 115. POST OFFICE BUILDING, 315 W. Pershing. Built in 1933. (photo 1976)

103

Fig. 116. FEDERAL COURTS BUILDING (and Post Office), Eighth to Ninth on Grand. Completed in 1939, Wight & Wight architects. (photo 1975)

Fig. 117. MUNICIPAL COURTS BUILDING, northeast corner of Locust and Twelfth. Completed in 1938, Wight & Wight architects. (photo 1977)

104

That was the last major governmental construction completed in the city in the 1930s.

Thus in a span of seven of the grimmest years of the Depression, exacerbated by the drought and the Dust Bowl, an intense program of government-sponsored construction altered large sections of older Kansas City. Six major buildings were added along with a number of lesser structures. There was the demolition of older buildings, and in the process the old civic center near Fifth and Main was radically changed while a new civic center was launched a mile to the south. One could see a formidable change in the appearance of the heart of the city as new public buildings joined recently completed office and store buildings. All of this had been done very quickly, at a speed of construction that surprises us today. The impact was considerable.

The new civic center was the most striking image of the changes that had taken place. There, three buildings were placed in calculated relationship to one another, and clad in a unified style of architecture. Except for some residential developments, and the commercial building of the Country Club Plaza, the city prior to that time had not had any significant exposure to this type of coordinated planning and the effect it could produce. Granted, the placement of the City Hall and the County Courthouse so that they faced each other across Twelfth Street was not a complicated piece of planning. But their bulk and stylistic affinity set up a dominant north-south axis which could provide the spine for a much more complex development, something suggested by the location of the Municipal Courts Building. Placed to the side, not in line with either of the larger structures, there was an implied minor, off-center, cross-axis, and with it the beginning of a civic plaza in the form of a monumental quadrangle. This did not evolve, however, despite later buildings added to that area.

The Courthouse, the first of the group, was the work of a team of architects headed by Wight & Wight, and included the firm of Keene & Simpson. Similarly, Wight and Wight were principals in the team that did the City Hall's design. And finally, Wight & Wight were responsible for the Municipal Courts Building. Hare & Hare, the preeminent landscape architects in Kansas City in this period, were also associated with the project. While it would be incorrect to call any of the buildings Neo-classic, since historic ornament as such was eliminated, the disciplined symmetry of the two principal buildings, the strong horizontal line created by the projecting lower stories that form the base out of which the shaft of the tower rises, the sculptured friezes, and the crisp, linear detailing, are all in the tradition of the Neo-classicism which Wight & Wight and other architects favored. A glance at Wight & Wight's earlier Neo-classic design, the Kansas City Life Building (Fig. 98), will show some important similarities in the massing and organization of at least the podium portion of the governmental structures.

The facade organization of the towers of the City Hall and the County Courthouse seems to have been influenced by the same trends that affected other high-rise buildings. So as in the Bryant Building, just two blocks west of the City Hall (Fig. 109), we can see a stressing of light-colored verticals through the use of darker window spandrels. The small stepbacks clustered near the top of the towers are similar in character to those used on the nearby Telephone Building (Fig. 100). And the use of a podium of lower stories, which provides a visual foundation for the tower, can be found on the Fidelity Bank (Fig. 107). These features also occurred on high-rises that were built throughout the nation and which were well publicized in the architectural journals of the day.

What is special in Kansas City is the incorporation of these features in a pair of government buildings of similar style which were sited to face each other. Also of interest is the way Art Deco ornament was given Neo-classic traits deemed appropriate for a public building. This is particularly well illustrated by the City Hall's lobby design (Fig. 111).

The failure to develop the simple but potentially majestic plan for the civic center is to be regretted, since the addition of buildings to the area after World War II not only ignored the original scheme, but actually obscured it to the point where later attempts to bring some harmony into the area have been abortive. Much of the later planning which has been suggested for the area has concentrated on the street grid and the traffic patterns as the dominant problem. What seems more important is the need to acknowledge that the basic axial plan did not center on the streets but rather at mid-block, and that the cross axis likewise did not fall along a street. Granted this mid-1930s plan ignored the possibility of increased automobile traffic through and around the area, nevertheless a meaningful expansion of the civic center could have taken place within the basic plan and could have worked despite increased automobile traffic.

What happened instead, was a location of subsequent buildings and the placement of surface parking lots which now suggests bigness without grandeur, and insularity of buildings rather than integration—a situation we will examine in greater detail in the next chapter. What is relevent to the present discussion is that the original plan, along with the original group of buildings, were based on Beaux-Arts concepts. These placed an emphasis on grand, formal arrangements in site planning and in the design of the buildings. The denial of this esthetic after World War II is the principal reason, in this writer's opinion, for the failure to develop the civic center either as an extension of the 1930s plan, or within any other viable concept for the center.

The placement of the Post Office on Pershing Road near the Union Station and Liberty Memorial represents a far more complicated problem than that at Twelfth and Oak. The station and the memorial, while placed across from one another, are not aligned axially and there is a significant difference in elevation between the two. Nevertheless, there is an effective pairing of the two structures, and the placement of any other building in the immediate vicinity creates quite a problem for the planner. The Post Office has the mass, the size, and the style to suggest that it was meant to be integrated with the earlier pair. But another building without any of these characteristics intrudes in the area and interrupts the visual interaction between the Post Office and the railroad station. But even if that intruder were removed, the orientation of the Post Office and its distance from the station would make it less of a match than is the much later Crown Center Hotel that now is an important addition to the architectural ensemble of that area. Perhaps the most important lesson to be learned from this grouping, and that of the civic center, is the near impossibility of resolving large scale planning when additions are conceived building by building, rather than in terms of implementing some overall plan. The latter provides guidelines which act to restrain, but not necessarily eliminate, individuality in design. At large scale, normal zoning regulations are only a partial answer to the problems implicit in developments implemented over a period of time. Large scale development represents a different degree of complexity than that which normally obtains in the usual course of city growth. This had become an issue of considerable importance in recent years when urban renewal escalated the role and the task of the city planner.

105

The site-planning problems associated with the construction of the Municipal Auditorium were minimal simply because they were deemed unimportant. Three major and several minor building functions were grouped within one enormous structure that occupied an entire city block. The massive building was put up without concern for other buildings in the area.

As we can see in Figure 114, the principal visual competitor in the 1930s was the Power and Light Building, and the latter was ignored. Indeed, given the location of the Auditorium and the orientation of the Power and Light, no realistic grouping was possible. The Auditorium Building was designed as a self-contained complex. On the lowest level, with its main entrance on Fourteenth Street, there is an exhibition hall surrounded by a mezzanine. Above that, there is an arena that can seat 14,000 people. The entrance of the arena, as well as those to the Music Hall and the Little Theatre, face Thirteenth Street, which lies at a higher elevation than Fourteenth, and thus provides direct access to the arena. Concealed behind the facade on Thirteenth Street is a theatre, the Music Hall, that can seat more than 2,500 people. It is placed so that it bridges across the Little Theatre, and the lobbies and promenades that serve the Music Hall and the arena. The Municipal Auditorium was built immediately south of the old Convention Hall which was then demolished.

After World War II the entire block on which it had stood was cleared, and a large underground garage and plaza was built. Unfortunately, the garage structure is not fully recessed below ground level, and as a consequence the plaza, which is elevated, does not provide the setting which was initially conceived for the limestone monumentalism of the auditorium. The choice of location for the auditorium, west of Wyandotte instead of near the civic center site, was partly dictated by the proximity of several major and many minor hotels as well as a long history of that section of downtown being an important entertainment and public assembly area.

The auditorium was a joint architectural effort of Gentry, Voskamp & Neville, with Hoit, Price & Barnes. They generated one of the finest Art Deco buildings in the city,

consistent throughout and down to the smallest detail (Fig. 113). The building's cost of $5,300,000 and the additional cost of site acquisition of $1,200,000, an impressive total in the early thirties, are an indication of the effort that was put into what was then one of the most modern and comprehensive convention and entertainment facilities in the nation.

The last major public building erected in the 1930s was the new Federal Courts Building, a design of Wight & Wight. The former building (Fig. 57) was razed in the winter of 1937-38, and the new building was completed on the same site in 1939. It is difficult to ascertain what influenced the architects to reduce their Neo-classicism to the extent that they did. The result is a building which is stark, with virtually no adornment, but which does exhibit Neo-classic proportions. The building is curiously unsatisfying and appears out of character for the architects. It is neither modern nor monumental. It is, however, big. While it is easy to point out what one perceives to be design flaws, the Federal Courts Building is nevertheless an important example of what was beginning to happen to architectural design in the late thirties. We are seeing the effect of a decade or more of growing accommodation to a modernist esthetic that was anti-historicism, and somewhat anti-ornamentation. As a major federal building, certain conservative traditions have lingered, but a new trend is also evident, one stressing an austere, uncluttered look that would be prevalent after the conclusion of World War II. In contrast to the embellished facade, the "new architectural look" rejects applied ornament—historic or otherwise—and relies on sheer planes, virtually no manipulation of shapes or textures, and shows little interest in a play of highlights and shadows. In this respect, the Federal Courts Building is an important transitional structure, though one suspects the neutering effect of an uninspired building committee as much as the influence of new esthetic theories.

The extent of the design change which is implicit in the Federal Courts is more apparent when we compare it with another Wight & Wight building completed a half dozen years earlier. This is the Nelson Gallery-Atkins Museum, which was opened to the public in 1933 (Fig. 118). The William Rockhill Nelson Gallery of Art and Mary Atkins

Fig. 118. NELSON GALLERY-ATKINS MUSEUM, 4525 Oak. View of the south facade. Completed in 1933, Wight & Wight architects. (photo 1977)

Museum of Fine Arts, to give it its full title, was designed in the tradition of a number of other art museums in the country. Located on the former estate of William Rockhill Nelson, at 45th and Oak, the Neo-classic features of the exterior, though restrained, are sufficiently pronounced to provide the symbolism then expected in the design of an art museum. Part monument, part temple to art, the art museum is also expected to be a vast storehouse, an exhibitions facility, a public assembly place, and an educational institution. Consequently, except for a few areas such as a great central hall, and an auditorium, the interior was designed as a large loft structure framed in reinforced concrete and steel which could then be divided and organized to provide for the many different functions that had to be served. The exterior design on the other hand was meant to suggest lasting artistic values, hence an appearance of timelessness was desired. This effect is achieved, more or less successfully, because we are willing to accept the symbolism inherent in Classic colonnades, rigid symmetry, stark limestone walls, reliefs and inscriptions. Put simply, the building looks like a museum. That it also functions quite well as an art museum, except that the public entrance is not on what appears to be the principal facade, is to the credit of Wight & Wight as well as later designers of the interior galleries.

More overt Neo-classic forms could have served the Federal Courts Building in much the same way and to the same objective, namely in being able to utilize an accepted image of monumentalism and solemnity that Neo-classicism then provided. This is illustrated by Keene & Simpson's Scottish Rite Temple at Linwood and The Paseo (Fig. 119), which was completed in 1930 and seems more in keeping with the tradition of federal structures than the 1939 structure on Grand. Monumentalism can be achieved in other ways of course, but the skinned look of the Federal Courts Building is not one of them.

The buildings of the new civic center would have provided an obvious opportunity to employ the emerging new esthetic, but even in that instance there was a hesitancy to make a full commitment. The design problem faced by architects in the 1930s was not a small one as they struggled to make use of the

Fig. 119. SCOTTISH RITE TEMPLE, northwest corner Linwood and the Paseo. Completed in 1930, Keene & Simpson architects. (photo 1974)

new architectural ideas while having to design buildings that related to a long tradition of familiar symbols and forms.

To return to the art museum, interest in creating such an institution in Kansas City had been long standing, but several ingredients had to be brought together before one could be built. The funds which had become available from the Nelson Trust were restricted to the purchase and direct care of art works. Thus the construction of a building to house the collection had to come from other sources, one of which was quite substantial, the Mary Atkins estate. Planning for the building began in the late twenties. The museum had its gala opening in December, 1933. Private philanthropy had launched a major art collection and had provided it with a suitable, controlled environment at a time when such large-scale construction had become almost exclusively the function of government patronage. What is remarkable is that in addition to this accomplishment, private philanthropy in Kansas City provided the start for two other important cultural institutions, a symphony orchestra and a university. So while the nation slipped ever deeper into the trough of the economic depression, Kansas City opened an art museum, organized a university, and started a symphony orchestra, all opening within a few months of each other late in 1933. The orchestra's initial performances were in the old Convention Hall, but it was scheduled to occupy the stage of the Music Hall in the Municipal Auditorium, soon to be constructed. That facility is still its principal home.

The university, considering the expectations held for it, began quite modestly in a mansion at 51st and Rockhill Road, which had been built in 1911 and which was a gift of William Volker, the university's greatest benefactor. There were early efforts to augment facilities, and three more buildings were added in 1935, 1936 and 1937. At this time the university was nothing more than a small liberal arts college with approximately 700 students, and the design of the new buildings was in keeping with that size and function. There were some attempts at "Collegiate Gothic" design, even though the mansion, the former Dickey home, was somewhat Renaissance in style. Design unity on the campus was achieved primarily through exterior walls that were built of rusticated stone in random ashlar pattern.

In 1939, William Volker gave the university $250,000 for a natural science facility. The Chemistry-Biology Building, now Fine Arts, designed by Charles A. Smith, was dedicated in 1942 (Fig. 120). Also in 1939, funds for a gymnasium were given by another donor, and it, too, continued the basic style of the campus.

It was in this time span that steps were taken to make the school a university in fact as well as in name. This was accomplished by the affiliation of three long-established, independent professional schools: Law in 1938, Dentistry in 1941, and Pharmacy in 1943. Despite this expansion in its first decade, the university remained small in its enrollments—a situation influenced in part by the war—and it remained financially strapped by the lack of a substantial endowment. It thus remained overly dependent on the annual benefactions of a few individuals, most notably William Volker. Generous as these were, his gifts were hardly adequate to create a second University of Chicago, the model that some wished to emulate in Kansas City. But within the context of a city that had never had a bona fide university, and limited

Fig. 120. FINE ARTS BUILDING (former Chemistry-Biology Building), Volker Campus, University of Missouri-Kansas City. Completed in 1942, Charles A. Smith architect. (photo 1955)

109

experience with any type of degree-granting college, the small group of stone buildings that represented the university appeared to be well launched and comparatively secure in its future. However, the University of Kansas City was facing a sizable economic crisis which was only temporarily delayed by the post-war surge in enrollments. The resolution of that crisis and the next stage of the architectural development of the university belong to later periods in our narrative.

In addition to the construction done for the university, the Kansas City, Missouri School District supported a building program in the 1930s. This consisted mostly of remodelings and additions to existing structures, but there were some new buildings. Southeast High School, on Meyer Boulevard at Swope Parkway, was perhaps the most impressive of the new buildings (Fig. 121). Started in 1936, the building by Wight & Wight is a compromise between English Gothic, school architecture, and the growing simplification of forms and details. It is interesting to observe the shift in style by the firm, from the Neo-classsicism we have seen them use, to one deemed appropriate to academe. Along with Smith's science

110

Fig. 121. SOUTHEAST HIGH SCHOOL, 3500 E. Meyer. Construction begun in 1936, Wight & Wight architects. (photo 1978)

could logically expect. But as those who can recall the 1930s from first-hand experience know, survival in the professions and in business was rooted in a much different value-system than that of today.

One factor that helped a number of architects to cope with the grim days of 1933-34 was their involvement in the Fort Peck Dam project on the upper Missouri River. A fairly large number of Kansas City architects were used to design various buildings, housing and support facilities required by the large numbers of workers on that project. About sixty people from Kansas City, including two women, were directly involved, so a photograph shows us. This was when there were fifty-six architectural firms with seventy-two principals listed in the City Directory.

At the start of the 1940s, there were other efforts to secure government-supported employment through a campaign to recruit for the area industrial plants needed to support the military buildup in the United States. War-related construction did increase in the region, and this did make use of the

building for the university, the high school illustrates the continued importance given to style-symbolism and some insight into why historic eclecticism held sway for so long. For many, the English Gothic, if tamed in certain ways, symbolized a hall of learning, even in the mid-1930s.

Patronage provided by governmental units and public institutions proved to be a major support for Kansas City architects during the 1930s; but there was private support as well, though severely reduced in scope. The overall volume of privately financed building in Kansas City dropped radically in the thirties, from over thirty million dollars in 1925 to only two million in 1935. The latter figure represents an upsurge after three really low years. Despite this decline, the number of architect's offices listed in the City Directories remained fairly high. So we must assume that the number of employees was severely reduced or simply restricted to the principals. These architects did receive commissions to do some new residences and an occasional church. They also did some commercial buildings, usually small structures. A sizable proportion of contracted services were apparently for renovations or modifications of existing buildings, or additions to them. If we add the governmentally supported work, the number of listed architects still seems larger than one

Fig. 122. BROOKSIDE THEATRE BUILDING, 6345 Brookside Plaza. Completed in 1937, severely damaged by fire in 1978, demolished in 1979. (photo 1976)

Fig. 123. Marquee of the BROOKSIDE THEATRE. (photo 1976)

was in keeping with an established local preference and thus not unusual. Lacking an adequate historic precedent for a theatre marquee over the cinema's entrance, a pure Art Deco design complete with colored lights and stylized lettering was created (Fig. 123). The building, which opened in 1937, sustained massive damage by fire early in 1978 and was demolished in 1979. In the Country Club Plaza, the Hispanic mode continued with the construction of the Alameda Tower Building, now Plaza Medical Building, in 1938 (Fig. 124).

Eclecticism was the norm in residential work, but here and there a number of homes were built in the mid-thirties in what was then called the "International Style." These vary in quality since so much depended on proportions and the massing of simple geometric forms. One of the very finest, and certainly the largest, is the 1936 Bixby Residence (Fig. 125) designed by Edward Tanner. He produced a considerable number of eclectic designs throughout the Country Club District and on the Plaza, but here he demonstrated his capabilities at modernism of the latest sort. The site of the Bixby House is on a slight rise of ground at 65th and State Line Road, and set within a ring of trees. The house is an excellent example of the style we associate with German

111

Fig. 124. PLAZA MEDICAL BUILDING (formerly ALAMEDA TOWER BUILDING), 300-block W. Nichols Road. Completed in 1937. (photo 1978)

architectural skills centered in Kansas City. And so in these various ways the profession was sustained through difficult years.

In private work completed in the 1930s, the tradition of historic eclecticism remained important in residential and church architecture. For the more limited commercial work, a goodly portion of it was also eclectic in style. The Brookside Theatre Building on Brookside Plaza near Meyer is a representative example (Fig. 122). The use of the Georgian style

112

Fig. 125. BIXBY RESIDENCE, 6505 State Line. Built in 1936-37, Edward W. Tanner, architect. (photo 1973)

architects of the period, such as Walter Gropius and Mies van der Rohe, both of whom would soon be at work in the United States.

Today, the term "International Style" is less frequently used, having given way to the twin designations of *Art Deco* and *Art Moderne*, the latter being a slightly later and more streamlined, more curvilinear variant of the former. Which of these designations might best apply to the Bixby Residence is open to personal interpretations, but this viewer sees it as an example of the Art Moderne. The same is true of the

Fig. 126. ROBINSON SHOE COMPANY BUILDING, 1016 Main. Remodeled facade and interior completed in 1936, James F. Terney architect. (photo 1976)

facade erected in 1936 for the Robinson Shoe Company at 1016 Main, by James F. Terney (Fig. 126). The stylized lettering, the lower portion of the projecting sign, the fluting at each side of the facade, the combination of a large window of glass brick and the large squares of glazed terra cotta, are representative of the Art Moderne style.

Thirteen years later, just down the street, the facade built by the newly arrived Macy's Department Store as part of their extensive remodeling of the former John Taylor store, would be a very late statement in this same esthetic (Fig. 127). Completed in 1949 by the firm of Kivett & Myers, the Macy's store anchored the west end of the two-block Petticoat Lane section of Eleventh Street. It was an important sign of architecture's resurgence after the conclusion of World War II. Other buildings or remodelings completed in the late 1940s made similar commitment to modernism, which meant for some simply a rejection of ornament. One of the most interesting, and certainly one of the finest designs of the late forties is that of the Catholic Church of St. Francis Xavier, at 52nd and Troost (Figs. 128 and 129). A 1948 design by Barry Byrne of Chicago, with Joseph B. Shaughnessy, Sr. of Kansas City associated, the plan of the church proper presents an outline reminiscent of a fish, the Early Christian symbol which represented Christ. The sleek geometry of the plan and of the masonry walls, and the absence of almost all ornament on the exterior except for the sculpture by Alfonzo Ianelli, mark this as an early example in the city of an alternative approach to church design, one not dependent on the symbolism of historic styles.

St. Francis Xavier was not the first Kansas City church to be an important, bold statement for modern architecture. There is the celebrated case of the Community Christian Church design by Frank Lloyd Wright at 46th and Main (Fig. 130). Wright tells his version of the controversy generated by the building of this church in his autobiography, in the section entitled "The Church of the Future." Designed in 1940, Wright had planned for a light steel frame, flexible in shape, resting on rock ballast foundations. The steel skeleton, which he called tenuous, was to be covered by heavy paper strung with steel wires (Steeltex) and then waterproofed with

113

114

Fig. 127. MACY'S DEPARTMENT STORE, 1034 Main. Comprehensive remodeling and redesign in 1949, Kivett & Myers architects. (photo 1978)

structure that extended and doubled the horizontal lines of the church proper. Nevertheless, some significant Wrightian characteristics remain, including the basic geometry of a hexagonal plan, and the cantilevered balconies and canopies.

Wright's difficulties may well have stemmed from having to deal with city departments that had a history of being mired in corruption. The political machine that held the city in its grasp was extending its influence in the late thirties beyond the city's limits. It was also bringing the city to the edge of bankruptcy. Efforts at reform had begun early in the 1930s, but the task was made difficult for there were padded voting rolls, which of course supported the machine, and there was voter intimidation generated by a bold underworld that was linked in various ways to key people in and behind the city's administration. However, aided by the evidence that Thomas J. Pendergast, the city's undisputed political boss who was thought to be personally honest, was himself guilty of income tax violations and accepting bribes, the reform movement succeeded. In 1939, Pendergast was sen-

Fig. 128. ST. FRANCIS XAVIER CATHOLIC CHURCH, 1001 E. 52nd. Built in 1948-50, Barry Bryne (New York) with Joseph B. Shaughnessy, Sr. architect. View from the northeast. (photo 1978)

sprayed cement (Gunite). The radical departures from the requirements of the city's building codes created a series of difficulties that finally led to Wright's withdrawal from the project. The building, which was completed under the supervision of Edward B. Delk of Kansas City, a well established and respected architect, was brought within the city's requirements and lost thereby some of the gracefulness of the original conception. This had included a parking

Fig. 129. ST. FRANCIS XAVIER CATHOLIC CHURCH. View from the east. (photo 1978)

Fig. 130. COMMUNITY CHRISTIAN CHURCH, 4601 Main. Designed in 1940 by Frank Lloyd Wright and completed by Edward B. Delk in 1941. (photo 1977)

116

tenced to the penitentiary, and in 1940 a new city government came into power. For the first time a professionally trained city manager, L. P. Cookingham, was in charge of day-to-day operations. The turnabout in the city's affairs was remarkable. In short order city finances were squared away and services were being augmented. This occurred just as new federal monies were being channeled into the city as a result of the industrial buildup that was generated by the United States' entry into World War II.

The mobilization of men and industry to support the war effort, however, left few resources available for the creation of architecture other than that directly associated with the prosecution of the war. Possibly the most significant local structure erected during the war—though then it lay just outside the city's limits—was an industrial building, the Pratt and Whitney aircraft engine plant on Bannister Road, east of Troost. Fifty-seven acres were placed under a single roof in 1943. Today it serves the Bendix Corporation.

Some housing was constructed during the war, and as with industrial plants, utility dominated stylistic niceties. With the conclusion of the hostilities, Kansas City prepared to enter a phase of development quite different from that of the preceding decades. The difficult years of the Great Depression were put behind though hardly forgotten, while efforts

were made to channel the economic buildup of the war years toward productive, peaceful ends. This, however, required a bit of time. As the transition from war to peace was implemented, as men returned to civilian life and controls were slowly lifted, new buildings appeared in the city. Their number, however, was not especially large. There were several reasons for this. In addition to the delays inherent in the retooling of the economy, the population of the city had not really grown very much since the late 1920s. Furthermore, though the implications for Kansas City were not immediately evident, there was renewed development in northeast Johnson County, Kansas, just to the west of the Country Club District, and that helped meet the city's needs for new housing. And then too, a modification was occurring in people's attitudes toward the older city.

For a considerable period, Kansas City had typically concentrated major commercial construction within clearly defined areas in and near the central business district or at well-established neighborhood locations at the intersection of major public transit routes. Industrial construction was placed on the basis of ready access to rail transport and water resources. Now in Kansas City, as elsewhere, these older centers of business and industrial activity were aging, and in some cases, deterioration had advanced to the point where demolition seemed necessary for renewal. This was different from the type of replacement-growth that had marked earlier downtown construction. That had been more akin to meeting the need for new clothing for a growing child. Now, after fifty to seventy years, entire sections of the urban core were seen as worn-out, not outgrown. Consequently a philosophy of redevelopment was formulated which received legislative support in 1947 at both the state and local levels. Plans were laid for redevelopment on Quality Hill, and in the area north of Ninth Street in downtown. These were coupled with plans for building limited access trafficways which would ring the central business district and ease automobile flow in and out of the older city. Further, plans were quietly developed to extend the city's limits through a programmed series of annexations that would prevent the aging city from being constricted by a younger, suburban ring, at least on the

Missouri side, as had happened to St. Louis.

One could not fault the logic of the plan, given the perceptions and the experience of that time, and indeed much of it can still be justified, especially in the light of the advantages generated by the implementation of the plans. A key to all of this was a successful vote for an annexation plan with only a simple majority required; and then the generation of support for a sizable bond program to build the city of the future was needed, a much more difficult task with the two-thirds requirement.

The annexation of nearly twenty square miles north of the Missouri River was approved in November, 1946, to take effect on January 1, 1950. It was the first of a series of annexations which would take the city to over 300 square miles in 1963. The bonds, to be expended over fifteen years,

were approved in November 1947. They consisted of sixteen city proposals for somewhat more than $41 million and five county proposals of slightly more than $6 million. The city's proposals represented some ambitious programs, including $6 million no-tax bonds that would permit a start on what has become Kansas City International Airport. Three days before the election, on behalf of four Clay County residents, a suit was filed which challenged the bonds on the premise that eventual annexation would obligate residents north of the river to pay taxes on issues on which they had not been permitted to vote, since annexation was not yet in effect. The suit tied up the sale of bonds until December 1949, when the city won its case. Thus the unexpected delay retarded the start of many key developments until 1950, when the long-standing boundary-barrier of the Missouri River would fall.

The arrival of Macy's Department Store, with its remodeled, updated building facade, symbolizes the character of the immediate post-war period. New and big, it was a welcome sign of growth and improvements in a city that was beginning to think boldly again. Other new structures used the same design esthetic, which was geometrically neat, clean cut, and virtually free of ornament. This is particularly evident in some of the apartment structures which were erected right after the war.

The Westport Central Apartments at 301 West Armour, designed by E. O. Bayerl in 1945, is a good example (Fig. 131). The use of two colors of brick, laid in simple, bold patterns, is coupled with a severity of overall design that emphasizes planes with sharply delineated openings and edges. This sums up the style that reached full expression in what was certainly the largest apartment complex of its time. This is the vast, two-building Twin Oaks Apartments at 50th and Oak (Fig. 132). Designed in 1949 by the firm of Voskamp & Slezak, each building is T-shaped, and though individual facades on Oak are asymmetrical, together they exhibit the formal balance typical of apartment buildings of the time. The facades are executed in two colors of brick, much as in the Westport Central Apartments. Here, too, there is a contrasting vertical emphasis provided by simulated pier

Fig. 131. WESTPORT CENTRAL APARTMENTS, 301 W. Armour. Designed in 1945, E. O. Bayerl architect. (photo 1978)

117

118

Fig. 132. TWIN OAKS APARTMENTS, 5000 and 5050 Oak. Completed in 1951, Voskamp & Slezak architects. (photo 1977)

buttresses at the inner ends of the two buildings. Placed on reclaimed land achieved through the straightening of Brush Creek along with the creation of Volker Boulevard in 1950, Twin Oaks was occupied in 1951.

Thus, with its size, its location, and its function, Twin Oaks along with the Macy's store, signal the revival of the city after lean and difficult years. Their construction coincided with the move to expand the size of the city and to add many new improvements. For many, the 1950s was expected to see the city back on its path toward hoped-for greatness, a destiny to be measured in part by large-scale modern architecture.

1950-1970
Retreat from the Past

In 1950 the city bustled with signs of progress. Annexation had finally taken the city across the river. Though there had been a small extension south to 85th Street in 1947, this was the first sizable addition to the city's area since 1909. The bonds which had been approved in 1947 were finally free from legal restraints, and they could be put to work now on a wide range of projects, augmenting activity already underway, such as the Southwest Trafficway. Land clearance under urban renewal had begun, and new buildings were beginning to appear on Quality Hill. With all of this and more going on, it was a propitious year for the city to celebrate its centennial, taking 1850, the year that the Town of Kansas was organized by County Court authority, as the "birth" of Kansas City.

To the centennial visitor, it would seem that the older city was being spruced up—modernized if you will—but without too many radical changes. For example, at the University of Kansas City a building for the School of Law was erected in 1950 on Rockhill Road at 52nd Street (Fig. 133). Since then, a new building for the School of Law has been erected. The first building, a design by the firm of Hardy & Schumacher, can be seen as a calculated compromise between tradition and modernism. It is more severely cubical than the university's other permanent buildings to that date (see Fig. 120). Since it was intended to relate to them, it was given rusticated stone walls and sculptured panels over the doors, while at the same time there was no attempt to continue the Collegiate Gothic style. Neither eclectic nor truly modern in style, the old Law School is representative of a good deal of post-war architec-

ture in the city, architecture which exhibited a tendency to avoid the cutting edge of the modernism contemporary to its time. In this respect, it forms a striking contrast to its near neighbor, St. Francis Xavier Catholic Church (Fig. 129), which was built in the previous year and is obviously less inhibited in its design.

If we look at the downtown architectural scene in 1950, we find the Centennial Building, by Frank E. Trask, at Tenth and Central (Fig. 134), as a major new structure. This office building, with enclosed garage, is more austere and more severely geometric than the university building, but here, too, no new design path is charted. In many ways it is a commercial variant of the massive, brick masonry of the Twin Oaks Apartments (Fig. 132). There is a bolder use of the brick which provides an illusion of strength in the masonry that is not as apparent in the apartment structures. Ornament is eschewed in both cases, and there is an emphasis placed on simple angular forms.

One of the most modern buildings built at this time is that for the American Hereford Association at Eleventh and Jefferson (Fig. 135). This 1951 design by Joseph Radotinsky is a clear break from the masonry conservatism of many post-war buildings. With its ribbon windows, projecting entrance, and openness of form, it is really quite different from most institutional or commercial buildings of that time. As the headquarters for an agribusiness-related organization, a moderate-sized building was sufficient, and full advantage was taken of the flexibility in planning that the modern style

Fig. 133. OLD LAW SCHOOL BUILDING, Volker Campus, University of Missouri-Kansas City. Built in 1950, Hardy & Schumacher architects. (photo 1977)

of architecture allowed and the site provided. The latter, in the urban renewal area of Quality Hill, is near the edge of the bluffs, located so that apartment houses are its nearest neighbors. Rectilinear massiveness and historical allusions were avoided by the architect, and the result is an overall lightness of design. The one out-of-character element is the later placement of the large plastic bovine on top of a pylon in front of the building. Like it or not, it reads as a commercial sign, albeit an unusual one, and this is out of place in the context of the building's design and location. The Quality Hill urban renewal project was the first phase in a larger program. It was the earliest indication in Kansas City of what could be expected from urban renewal that was intended to clear away aged and deteriorated buildings, and to replace them with structures that would provide a significant upgrading of the area. The change in the appearance of the buildings was radical (compare Figs. 135 and 23).

Now, more than twenty years later, one finds the overall planning of the site to be rather conventional except for the retention of the lookout areas and the park at the edge of the

Fig. 135. AMERICAN HEREFORD ASSOCIATION BUILDING, 715 W. Eleventh (Hereford Drive). Designed in 1951, Joseph Radotinsky architect. (photo 1978)

121

bluffs, features that had their origin with George Kessler, the city's great planner for its parks and boulevards.

With the advantage of today's hindsight, we can see that the Quality Hill plan and the buildings of 1949-51 summarize the principal traits one can find in the architecture of the early fifties. There is no sweeping surge of innovation. Rather, there was a cautious movement toward an increased modernism in architecture that did not make too many demands on an inherently conservative clientele. While city planning and the design of buildings in the early fifties moved the city gently forward without serious challenge to established conventions, there were some other circumstances that proved to have an unsettling effect on the city and this eventually affected its architecture.

First, there was the great flood of 1951. On Friday, July 13, after weeks of heavy rain, the dikes along the Kaw were breached by the swollen stream. By the time the waters receded, property damage on both sides of the state line near the mouth of the Kaw was estimated to be nearly one billion

Fig. 134. CENTENNIAL BUILDING, 234 W. Tenth. Designed in 1950, Frank E. Trask architect. (photo 1978)

dollars. The industrial heart of the metropolitan area was severely damaged. Restitution of the ravaged bottoms diverted attention and capital that otherwise might have been channeled into new construction.

Then, too, there was the Korean War. Hostilities began in the summer of 1950, and the military buildup with all of its economic implications was having its impact by the following summer. Truce was not established until the summer of 1953. The flood and the war, however, were not the only ingredients in the mix that was affecting architecture in the 1950s. Another was the attitude of the bureaucratic structure that administered the FHA and GI loans for the purchase of homes. Applications relative to houses in the new developments ringing the older city were treated far more favorably than those for older residences in established and now aging neighborhoods, especially if the latter were near sections that housed the Black community. This attitude was of a piece with the one that favored easing the flow of traffic to and from the suburbs through a radiating set of freeways and other traffic arteries that were charted through older neighborhoods. This, in and of itself, was considered neither wrong nor poor planning, for in an earlier age a network of streetcar lines helped decentralize this and other cities, and made way for a rapidly growing urban population. What was different was the fact that the distribution of the population was now actively assisted by government policy and practice, and the roads were not speculative franchises. Government practice favored the new over the old, a prejudice that was hardened in a rather peculiar way by the landmark legal decision that voided governmentally sanctioned racial segregation in the public schools.

Until 1954, Missouri maintained a mandated dual public school system, a system that severely limited the Black population in Kansas City in its educational options. This, in turn, was matched by a rather tightly demarcated pattern of residential segregation that placed the overwhelming majority of the Blacks in the city between 9th and 27th Streets, and from Holmes to Prospect. There were several other enclaves, but virtually no Blacks lived south of 31st, or in the northeast section of the city. Only one high school, Lincoln, served this

population which was also restricted by a host of social and economic practices that limited public access, accommodation, and employment.

The 1954 Supreme Court decision had little immediate impact on either the schools or residential segregation. A Public Accommodations Ordinance was not passed in Kansas City until 1964. One reason for the slowness of change was the inertia under which the schools and the community operated in matters of social behavior. Another factor was grounded in the way the several school districts of the state are delineated and supported. From this arose a peculiar situation that was in the long run to have a profound influence on the demography of the city, and thus its architecture. School district boundaries are drawn independently of the political boundaries of the various municipalities, though these often did, in fact, coincide. Therefore, when the city annexed portions of Clay County in 1950, the Kansas City, Missouri School District did not follow. The 1957 annexation to the east of the 1909 limits did not alter the school district's limits in that direction, and so forth. The result is that Kansas City, Missouri is served by a number of separate and quite independent school districts, none of which, other than the Kansas City, Missouri district itself, has had much if any experience or interest in serving a Black population. In fact, the Kansas City, Missouri School District had served as a regional, segregated education service on the Missouri side of the state line. It became clear very quickly that there was a widespread intention, unwritten to be sure but definitely understood, that this practice was expected to continue whatever the Supreme Court had decided.

The closer a neighborhood, and thus its schools, was to Black residential areas, the less favorably was it considered for FHA and GI loans. This became a much more complicated matter in the late fifties when the new freeway system angled Interstate 70 through the historic Black community and displaced a large number of residents, thus breaking the traditional limits that had enclosed this population. The resettlement was channeled by a variety of practices to funnel Blacks to the south and southeast of the historic district. Even though ready money was available to purchase new homes, because former residences were condemned and bought outright, it was virtually impossible for Blacks to buy except in areas that were somehow identified as within the accepted channel for migration. This was accompanied by block-busting tactics and outright discriminatory practices that are all too familiar to urban residents. Residential segregation was continued and even strengthened by what is termed as White Flight.

One can, of course, misinterpret the evidence and impressions produced by such a volatile situation as the Black migration and in-migration that affected Kansas City but not the surrounding communities except for Kansas City, Kansas. But some facts stand out clearly and obviously. Except for the two Kansas City School Districts, enrollment of minorities is not significant in the other districts of the greater metropolitan area. Redlining in home loans and insurance became a sufficiently widespread practice to draw official comment, and that meant there were no loans or insurance coverage, or only under very unfavorable conditions, available to large sections of the older city. This, of course, affected the decisions of prospective property owners, and it limited the ability to maintain properties held by people with limited capital. Racial minorities remain mostly residentially segregated within the metropolitan area, to a large degree within certain sections of the city itself. Efforts to ameliorate this have been confounded by a host of factors. While some progress has been made to break down old habits and beliefs, racial segregation is still very much a part of the Kansas City, Missouri residential scene.

The suburbs and the outlying areas of the city were seen by many as a haven in the sixties, at least from the point of view of escaping the impact of having to cope with public schools that were rapidly increasing their numbers of minority students. A great many White families were simply not prepared to deal with that situation, especially when outlying school districts were perceived as providing superior educational programs. Today, it is not at all uncommon for executives and professionals arriving in the city to be informed that they should avoid living within the area served by the Kansas City, Missouri School District unless they

could send their children to private schools.

Segregation, desegregation, resegregation, and the status and quality of the various schools are not the principal subjects of this history, important as they might be. What is germane in all of this is that these issues affected large numbers of individual decisions that led to what amounted to a writing-off of a large section of the inner city. This had a major role in the developing architectural future of the city except as it served certain urban renewal or freeway planning situations.

If we concentrate on the architectural implications, we can see why residential patterns changed. We have a partial explanation for the population decline that began to affect the area within the limits set in 1909, and later within a widening ring beyond the limits of the Kansas City, Missouri School District. None of this was abrupt. Rather, it was gradual and apparently inexorable. Business and then industry began to follow the people. This, too, affected the

123

Fig. 136. THE LANDING SHOPPING CENTER, partial view from the southwest, 63rd to Meyer Blvd. at Troost. Opened in 1961, Edward Tanner architect. Enclosed in 1968. (photo 1978)

architecture of the city, something one can begin to see in the late 1950s, becoming more pronounced in the 1960s. Business follows the more affluent, and the migration of retail businesses and personal service professionals was away from the central business district and from the established neighborhood shopping centers, except for the Country Club Plaza. Shopping malls and specialized professional buildings that could provide ample, free parking, and which were closer to the newer residential areas, received the migration.

An early example of this type of development is The Landing (Fig. 136), which opened in 1961 on a tract of land east of Troost between 63rd and Meyer Boulevard. Originally an open air mall of about twenty-nine retail stores and outlets, it was not too far removed in character from a conventional group of shops that would face each other across a street, except that automobile traffic was confined to the perimeter of the tract. The mall was enclosed and air conditioned in 1968, and just recently there has been a major

interior renovation to keep it competitive with the much larger enclosed centers in more outlying areas. This pattern of regular improvements and changes is typical of this type of facility. The original design was by Edward W. Tanner.

As the number of shops and offices downtown and in the old neighborhood centers declined, entertainment facilities began to suffer from the reduced traffic. When the added burden of television was received, they, too, began to fold. Empty store fronts, empty offices, closed theatres marked the older business centers by the end of the 1950s, and with this came a growing neglect of buildings. Add the peculiarities of how property taxes are assessed, which seemed blind to the realities of the post-Korean War urban migration, and building demolition became an attractive alternative to building neglect. The changes were real and they would prove to be telling, especially when seen from our vantage point two decades later. In the 1950s the trends were less obvious. There was evidence that seemed, in fact, to suggest that the older

124

Fig. 137. MIDWEST RESEARCH INSTITUTE, 425 Volker Blvd. First unit designed in 1953, Neville, Sharp & Simon architects. (photo 1977)

city was being renovated in a manner to ensure a promising future as the heart of a great metropolitan area.

The Midwest Research Institute, established in 1943 and supported primarily through its research grants, had prospered to where it could build its own home, on Volker Boulevard at Oak (Fig. 137), not too far from the Twin Oaks Apartments. A 1953 design of Neville, Sharp & Simon, it was sited so that it faced, over a considerable distance, the Nelson Gallery-Atkins Museum (Fig. 118). As a consequence of its prominent location, and its distant pendant, the building's facade is severely symmetrical, but in no way Neo-classical. Except for the facade enframement in stone, the cladding of the long, horizontal structure follows the modern mode of the early 1950s. The Volker facade is a clear expression of the curtain wall, using glass and thin metal members. The rest of the exterior was clad in brick. The thin geometry of the curtain wall on Volker seems a bit constrained by the visually heavy weight of the stone frame, the latter no doubt intended to match the masonry of the Nelson Gallery. In this respect the design does not quite succeed, and since the addition of a second unit on Volker, which is almost the same exterior design, the visual interaction between the institute and the museum is negligible.

A more successful expression of this style, and a far larger and more interesting building, is the headquarters for Hallmark Cards Incorporated, at 25th and McGee Trafficway (Fig. 138). A 1950 design by the Los Angeles architect, Welton Becket, the building was completed in 1955. Here there is great size but without the appearance of bulk, and there is a more constructivist approach to design. Glass curtain walls are not given heavy enframements, and the use of metal on the exterior is frank and direct. Of the buildings of the period, this is certainly one that has aged very well, and it has not become dated in appearance, being able to hold its own against the context of the later architecture of Crown Center (Figs. 173 to 179).

The building at 3430 Broadway, built for the Old Security Life Insurance Company (Fig. 139), is another design that has managed to handle the passage of time without difficulty. Built in 1959, it is a Kivett & Myers & McCallum design.

Fig. 138. HALLMARK CARDS INCORPORATED headquarters building, 25th and McGee Trafficway. Designed in 1950 and completed in 1955. Welton Becket (Los Angeles) architect. (photo 1976)

125

Partial sunscreens, some distance in front of the curtain walls of glass, are supported by thin vertical members that set up a light, even delicate appearance, which manages to avoid a feeling of weakness. Careful proportions and the rigid geometric patterning contribute to this success. This building is a fine example of the use of exterior screening, a design feature that was popular at this time. The building itself is one of the most successful in the series of office buildings that were erected on Broadway, between 31st and 39th, during this period.

The final example in this brief review of 1950s office buildings, is the Old American Insurance Company at 4900 Oak (Fig. 140). Situated to the immediate west of the Midwest Research Institute, across Oak, this design by Voskamp and Slezak consists of two identical three-story blocks, one facing Oak and the other Volker, and a taller, recessed block that joins them and faces on Oak. Here there is a stone enframement of the curtain walls, but the proportions are far more subtle than on the research institute. The constructivist approach to the three-block grouping provides an interest that an otherwise simple rectangular block would

126

Fig. 139. OLD SECURITY LIFE INSURANCE BUILDING, 3430 Broadway. Built in 1959, Kivett & Myers & McCallum architects. (photo 1977)

not likely have. The building was ready for occupancy in 1959.

These four buildings, each representing an important commitment to the older city, were not, however, built in the central business district. That area was not neglected, but its development in the middle to late fifties proceeded along a path that was complex due to urban renewal, freeway construction, and some rather ambitious planning. For example, there was the concerted effort to ease access to the central business district and to provide additional pay parking. Two bridges across the Missouri River were completed: the Paseo Bridge in 1954 and the Broadway Bridge in 1956. Farther east, the Chouteau Bridge had been converted to vehicular traffic.

Fig. 140. OLD AMERICAN INSURANCE COMPANY BUILDING, 4900 Oak. Completed in 1959, Voskamp & Slezak architects. (photo 1976)

In town, the very large Auditorium Plaza Garage was completed in 1955 (see Fig. 114). These visible and important signs of central city development were, however, also aids to the decentralization of the city, something that would increase year by year. The citizenry was becoming more and more dependent on the private automobile, the essential ingredient to make the suburbs and the outlying sections of the city viable bedroom communities. Reliance on the automobile was at the expense of public transportation. The termination of streetcar service in 1957 can be taken as a sign of the problems faced by public transit which they tried, with little success, to resolve.

Also in 1957, work was progressing on the Sixth Street Expressway which was to be the north arm of the depressed freeway loop around the central business district (Fig. 141). The loss of the street railways could be offset by increased use of buses. But the freeway eliminated a great many buildings and permanently removed a large section of land from further architectural use as is made so evident in the view of the expressway.

It was in 1957, a year of changes and development, that the Kansas City Chapter of the American Institute of Architects

produced a massive study of the downtown area. Called KC/80, the work was summarized in a large model of the central business district. Starting with the givens of the great freeway loop and the bridges that crossed the river, large areas of new construction were plotted to provide for a modern, vital urban core. Historic preservation, however, had no significant role in Kansas City planning in the late 1950s. For that matter, not until the late 1960s was there a large enough collective concern to make the issue felt. Consequently, it was not uncommon to see planning proposals for downtown that simply eliminated many older buildings or hid them behind depersonalized veneers. The objective was to make over large sections of the downtown area. There was an enormous amount of faith that this would be realized and that the results would be a great improvement.

As a case in point, the public library after many crowded years was able to move in 1959 to a new facility at Twelfth and Oak, just west of the County Courthouse (Fig. 142). Large, modern, and more conveniently located, the new

127

Fig. 141. SIXTH STREET EXPRESSWAY, looking east from the Wyandotte viaduct. (photo 1976)

Fig. 142. PUBLIC LIBRARY AND BOARD OF EDUCATION BUILDING, 311 E. Twelfth. Completed in 1959, Edward W. Tanner architect. (photo 1978)

128

library and office building for the school district proved to be a good illustration of what the new planning was intended to achieve. There was no question that in many respects the new library was a fine facility. The buildings it displaced were nowhere near as impressive or appropriate to the area of the civic center. However, the new library building also illustrates a problem that would grow more acute, namely the problem of reconciling the style of new buildings with the style(s) of older ones in the area. For years this problem had been ignored with varying results. In the case of the library and the civic center, the problem was more pressing. For this was the first, sizable government/public building to be added to the center since the Courthouse, the City Hall, and the Municipal Courts Building had been built. As it stands, the library is a rather awkward visual addition to the mid-thirties civic center. It does not extend the basic plan for the complex, as previously discussed, and though some limestone is used for a podium of lower stories to support a short, massive tower of metal and glass, the library neither contin-

ues nor really complements the style of the older buildings. The lower stories of the library are proportionally smaller and more open than the corresponding sections of the older buildings. The library is placed much closer to Twelfth Street than is the County Courthouse to its east. Designed by Edward W. Tanner, it is, however, very definitely modern in appearance for its period. This provided valuable, symbolic significance for a community that had been told over and over again that the library on Ninth (Fig. 58) was woefully out of date as well as overcrowded.

One can speculate endlessly on the problem of an alternative design for the library, one that would produce the appropriate symbolism and be better integrated into the 1930s core of the civic center, but our concern is with what was built. And that tells us that not only was the design work of the late-nineteenth and early-twentieth century to be left behind, but now also that of the 1930s. The past would, of course, receive some acknowledgments, but it is clear that the present was not to be subservient to it. In this sense, the attitude is really an extension of nineteenth century individualism, but now clad in austere geometric raiment of the 1950s.

The same was occurring in multi-unit residential architecture. Just north of the original cluster of Country Club Plaza buildings (Figs. 77 and 78) a high-rise apartment structure, the Parkway Towers (Fig. 143) was going up concurrently with the new library. Designed by Herbert E. Duncan in 1959, the Parkway Towers is in fact one of the more sensitively conceived apartment buildings designed in the period, avoiding a harshness of form and of facade organization that many others, sadly, did display. But in its scale, geometry, and avoidance of ornament, it is definitely at variance with the older buildings near it. Having said this, we must add that we are not advocating that there be no changes from established, older styles. Rather, the point is that there is a problem in how one does relate a new building stylistically to the architecture that forms its immediate surroundings. The challenge of this problem is a real one, and there are many examples where it has been met successfully, and without recourse simply to continuing the style of older buildings.

Fig. 143. PARKWAY TOWERS, 4545 Wornall. Designed in 1959, Herbert E. Duncan architect. (photo 1978)

However, the history of urban architecture in America has many more examples where this is not the case. In the late 1950s, it was not seen as a critical issue. The symbolism implicit in an up-to-date building exterior was enormously important, and the period of the late fifties and early sixties seems the high point in this attitude in Kansas City. Interestingly enough, it also seems to be the period with the lowest interest in historic eclecticism, certainly much lower than is the case for the late sixties and the seventies.

The most impressive urban symbol of architectural modernism in the fifties in the United States was the high-rise office or apartment tower. There were a number of the latter that had been built in Kansas City, such as the Parkway Towers. However, there were no high-rise office buildings erected in the fifties, or the forties for that matter. The symbol of progress, the tall office building, was conspicuously absent from Kansas City's architectural record of the 1940s and 50s. With the advantage of hindsight, one can suggest some possible explanations. One frequently mentioned is the

paucity of large, national firms headquartered in Kansas City, firms of the sort that would see the modern office tower as a suitable corporate image. Hallmark Cards Incorporated is hardly Standard Oil or U.S. Steel, but it too is a leader in its field. It built a large office building in Kansas City (Fig. 138), but it was not built downtown, and it certainly is not a high-rise.

The same occurred with other locally-based companies. The symbolism was not needed apparently. The unwillingness of investors to risk construction capital in or even near blight-ridden neighborhoods—presumably most of downtown—and the fiscal conservatism of community leaders have been suggested as reasons for the office towers missing from the construction done in the 1950s. Whatever the reasons and their pertinence, the fifties were slow in this sense. There was a turn-around in attitude in the sixties, and finally some new high-rise office space began to appear.

The first was the Traders Bank tower (Fig. 144) at Twelfth and Grand. A design of the Dallas architect Thomas E. Stanley, this high-rise was completed in 1963, twenty-six years after the last high-rise, City Hall, had been built. While hardly a giant, either in area or height, the twenty-story slab, three by seven bays, was indeed the first noticeable addition to a skyline that had seemed immutable for a full generation. The exterior, above the banking and garage levels, is a simple grid with little variation on the exterior except for an offset, brick elevator/service shaft at the northwest corner, and large graphics at the roof level. Neither is visible in the illustration. If the bank were located near the City Hall, it would be as much a contrast as is the library, but in its location on Grand its visual competitors are such buildings as the Professional Building (Fig. 103), the Bryant Building (Fig. 109), and the Federal Reserve Bank (Fig. 91). While these are obviously different in style, they do bear certain similarities in their organization of the facades, with strong verticals in the case of the first two, and with clean-cut window openings and counterbalancing horizontals in the case of the third. Furthermore, all four are corner-lot structures, with Grand Avenue the linking feature, the axis that draws one from one to the other. There is no Beaux-Arts formalism in their

129

130

Fig. 144. TRADERS NATIONAL BANK, northeast corner of Twelfth and Grand. View looking west on Twelfth. Completed in 1963, Thomas E. Stanley, Inc. (Dallas) architect. (photo 1977)

interrelationship to emphasize their visual differences.

The construction of the Traders Bank downtown was a reminder of how centripetal the city's growth had been. The center had received considerable attention in the form of freeway construction and land clearance, but not a great deal of important new construction. It was becoming questionable if the center could provide a counterbalance to the develop-

ing perimeter. For example, the metropolitan area, and especially downtown, had seen virtually no new hotel or motel construction in the decade following the end of World War II, though a slight expansion of an existing downtown hotel did take place.

On some of the major highways there were some motels, but their number was smaller than one might expect, and their distribution was rather uneven. The growing use of the automobile for intercity travel had put pressure on hotels to provide convenient, free parking, a resource not readily available to older hotels. Thus new hotel construction in the downtown area was in the form of multi-story motor inns. Land clearance and the developing freeway network made this feasible and several were constructed in the late 1950s, providing a modicum of counterbalance to those added at the perimeter of the metropolitan area.

Motel designs by the late fifties were becoming standardized, but on occasion there was a significant variation from formula as in the case of the one that finally opened as the Hilton Inn Cliff House at Seventh and Washington. It is now the Ramada Central. A 1959 Kivett & Myers design, it has undergone some changes, but the exterior configuration is still much as it was when built (Fig. 145). No large-scale hotel, however, with or without motor inn aspects was being built at this time in the central portion of the city.

As the sixties matured, serious considerations were given to the construction of new, convention-size hotels as well as to improved convention and exhibition facilities. This was part of an awakening to the full implications of the fact that Kansas City now had some major competitors for conventions and meetings, activities that were important to the continued business health of the central business district.

The city had not kept pace with many other medium-sized cities in the nation in the construction of new facilities and attractions which would persuade decision-makers to think of Kansas City as the place to which they should relocate, or in which to meet. The convenience for passengers of the airport near downtown was a strong plus. For the airlines which were converting to jet aircraft, a larger and more remote airport was becoming an important safety feature which offset this advantage. Municipal Auditorium, an extraordinary facility in the mid-thirties, was less and less able to meet the changes in demands, mostly for larger exhibition and meeting spaces. Despite the enlargement and renovation of hotels and some new construction, the convention bureau was told repeatedly that there were not enough first-class hotel rooms in close proximity to one another and to convention facilities to meet current demands. Everything was not up to date in Kansas City, and the point was repeatedly driven home. The Metropolis of the Midlands—if that was the civic goal—was not a major league city when it came to conventions. The city was being measured by more criteria than simply the size of its population or its area.

Important to many was the fact that the city lacked big league sports, a situation that a number of city and business leaders worked to rectify. Success came in 1955 with the transfer of an American League baseball team from Philadelphia to Kansas City. After its subsequent loss to Oakland, the city gained an expansion team, the Royals, who have become

Fig. 145. RAMADA CENTRAL (formerly Hilton Inn Cliff House), 610 Washington. Designed in 1959, Kivett & Myers architects. (photo 1978)

powerful contenders. In 1963, the Dallas team of the American Football League moved to Kansas City, becoming the Chiefs, the first of its league to play in the Super Bowl. The city's image was improving in some eyes, but with little effect on the city's architecture. Initially, both teams played in a refurbished, former minor league, baseball stadium. In time, handsome new facilities were constructed.

At the other end of the major league image, but very much a part of what a city is and must do, was the growing problem of housing the urban poor. During the Pendergast period, the attitude of city officials was that there was no need for public housing. It was true that the vast acreages of deteriorating tenements of the type found in New York or Chicago did not exist in Kansas City. However, a large number of people did live in sub-standard and aging housing, and this was recognized by the reform government. Some low rent public housing had been built during World War II and during the Korean War, but the bulk of the city's public housing was constructed at the end of the fifties and the early sixties. Most of this was located as replacements for older, decayed housing stock, and with one major exception, it consisted of groupings of small structures. Kansas City did erect one large-scale, high-rise complex called Wayne Miner which has had its problems as have similar facilities elsewhere. Public housing can and does vary in the quality of its design. In most instances in the city, the examples from this period exhibit no distinctive features that would single them out for special consideration here. But then that is true of a great many of the detached houses for single-family occupancy that were built in the city throughout the two decades of this period.

Some large, architect-designed residences were being built, but it seems that with few exceptions the best of these were erected outside of the city limits, mostly in northeast Johnson County, Kansas. Two of these exceptions are the house the architect Albert J. Yanda designed for himself at 1102 Valentine Road (Figs. 146 and 147), and the Nicol House designed by Bruce Goff at 5305 Cherry (Fig. 148).

Both were built in 1966, and interestingly enough, both were built in old, established neighborhoods. Despite these innovative solutions to residential architecture, and some

131

Fig. 146. ALBERT J. YANDA RESIDENCE, 1102 Valentine Road. View from the south. Completed in 1966, Albert J. Yanda architect. (photo 1976)

132

buildings, and in commercial, industrial and institutional work, not in the small, residential designs that were being executed.

For various reasons, the detached house failed to capture the imagination and the time of the willing patron, the gifted designer, and the searching critic to the extent that it had formerly. But even more to the point, the overall quality of design one finds in the tract-type house built after World War II is not very interesting visually or spatially. In many ways, it is inferior to its equivalent built before the war. Shifting values, climbing costs, and changing patterns of taste seemed to reduce the bulk of post-war residential design to formula appliques, always granting the inevitable exceptions. Regrettably, we must note that they do appear to be exceptions.

If we take the longer view, we can see that a great period of residential design began in the city during the real estate boom of the middle 1880s. It continued well into the depression years, a total period of about fifty years. By the mid-1930s, restraints pretty well affected all architecture. Since World War II, single-family residential work appears to

others in the city, the majority of detached houses built after World War II have been cautiously designed. They are rather predictable in appearance in that they either extend, in watered-down fashion, older styles into the present, or are variants of what quickly became known as the Ranch Style. A cliff-hugging house of the sort that we see in the Yanda House, with its frank expression of structural steel supports, was somewhat limited in its appeal in Kansas City. The circular plan, unusual silhouette, and decorative features of the Nicol House were no more likely to attract widespread imitation. The problem, of course, was that residential architecture which deviated too much from traditional configurations was difficult to finance, and while there were some excellent residential designers, the opportunities afforded them to be truly creative seemed to shrink even as the city grew. Further, if one studies the publications that feature the accomplishments in American architecture of the late 1940s through the fifties and sixties, we find that critics and historians stressed achievements in large-scale residential

Fig. 147. YANDA RESIDENCE, view from the west. (photo 1976)

Fig. 148. JAMES NICOL RESIDENCE, 5305 Cherry. Completed in 1966, Bruce Goff architect. (photo 1976)

becoming prohibitively expensive by the 1950s. We have already mentioned the decline that affected architectural terra cotta. Our point is not to suggest that these craft skills were no longer extant. Fine craftsmen did and still do exist. Rather, the number of these people had been radically reduced. The cost of their work had escalated to where one could not automatically include design and detailing of the sort they could do and know it could be executed within the budget allowed. Long-held traditions within the building trades were changing, and architects now had to work within this realization. The changes that we see then were not simply the result of a new building esthetic, though there was a rising opposition to historic eclecticism, a design mode that made extensive use of fine millwork, masonry, etc., but also a reaction to influences far removed from issues of architectural taste.

133

Residential design is not confined, of course, to detached houses, which were less and less the individualized work of identified architects. There is also multiple-unit residential construction. Though there was a fairly steady program of tract-home construction in the fifties and sixties, in the case of apartment house construction, there was an extraordinary surge which occurred in the middle 1960s. Here we find a great variety of designs, particularly in the type known as garden apartments, and with apartment buildings, the designers are known. After the flurry of post-war building of apartments, which included the Twin Oaks complex, such construction sagged, with very little action from 1955 through 1957. Whether this reflected economic influences, or a general conviction that more new apartment units were not needed, or were not popular, or a combination of these, we cannot say. The evidence is clear that 1955 was a real low point in post-war multi-family residential construction in the city. A slow revival began at the end of the fifties and this grew stronger until 1964 and 1965, when almost as many apartment units were being built as were single-family residences. This surge finally terminated in 1973, at a time when the inflation in building costs, and the rising expense of construction financing, had reached a point where fair-return rentals had all but priced this type of building, if newly

have mutated to the place where one cannot find the post-war equivalent of a streetscape of the sort still visible in the older sections of town, as in the Valentine-Roanoke area, or along lower Ward Parkway, or in the Sunset Hill district. The difference is not in size or in design consistency, rather it is in the type of detailing and in the use of materials.

One factor affecting the change—and this applies to more than architecture—is the range and extent of the skills available in the several crafts, skills that helped make earlier residential designs inimitable today if tried in any quantity. One still remembers the sad tale told in 1950 at a stoneyard in central Illinois. The owner lamented his inability to find a single person willing to learn the craft of hand-stonecarving, even under the GI Bill. And he recognized that when his remaining aged stonecarver, who had received his training in Italy, retired, he would no longer be able to provide a service that once was routinely expected in almost any city of size. The same was happening in the areas of wood working and fancywork bricklaying. If the skill was available, it was

built, out of the market.

In general, the construction of new apartments during the sixties followed one of three approaches. First, there was the development of a sizable tract of land, using a number of apartment buildings of two or three stories, sometimes with what are called townhouses included. Distributed over a sizable site, possibly using several basic building designs but more typically a repeated pattern, these large developments included off-street parking, swimming pools, club houses, and other amenities.

134

The complex called The Mews, at 97th and Lydia (Figs. 149 and 150), which had sixty-six units ready for occupancy in 1966, with later additions, is representative of the category. It is a Linscott, Kiene & Haylett design. While basically simple in style, using brick with wood for exterior staircases and balconies, the variation in arrangement and placement of buildings, some in handsome settings, and the concern for a full circumferential design of each structure, has made this a more interesting complex than a view of a single building

Fig. 150. THE MEWS APARTMENT COMPLEX, partial view. (photo 1978)

Fig. 149. THE MEWS APARTMENT COMPLEX, a general view, 97th and Lydia. Initial group of units completed in 1966, Linscott, Kiene & Haylett architects. (photo 1978)

might otherwise suggest.

Large groupings such as The Mews are more typically found in the newly annexed areas, or in new suburban developments, than within the older city. In the latter case, one finds our second category of apartment construction, the small-area redevelopment. Here, a group of contiguous, single-family dwellings usually is razed to provide space for one or more apartment structures. Depending on the mix of circumstances, the result might range from a rather small, simple building with just a few units, to a fairly complex arrangement that would also include swimming pool, saunas, off-street parking and such. The structure at 3634 Warwick, called Chateau 37 (Fig. 151), is a representative example. It was designed by Terry Chapman, and it was completed in 1965. It differs in its choice of materials and appearance from the buildings of The Mews, and is but one version of a type of building that ranged quite widely in style at this time, from the austere contemporary look, to the rustic, to revivals of historic eclecticism. Some are beyond stylistic definition other than calling them, charitably, "failed fantasies."

Fig. 151. CHATEAU 37 APARTMENTS, 3634 Warwick. Completed in 1965, Terry Chapman architect. (photo 1978)

Fig. 152. THE REGENT APARTMENTS, 1111 W. 46th. Completed in 1965, Linscott, Kiene & Haylett architects. (photo 1978)

136

One could expand the number of examples, and we would see a wide variety of designs—in some ways more extensive than those we would find in single-family houses of the period—but no additional insight would be gained. The Chapman design illustrates the way in which architects strove to introduce visual interest through variations in what is basically a repetition of selected, modular designs. The real challenge was to avoid the anonymity that one finds in the two and three-story apartment buildings that are simple, red brick boxes that are ornamented, if at all, only with simulated Georgian doorways.

The third category of apartment building is one already alluded to, these are the high-rise buildings which can be found in a variety of locations, on Quality Hill, near the Country Club Plaza, and elsewhere where zoning permitted this density of residential construction.

One motivation in the generation of this type of dwelling-structure seems to have arisen in the late-fifties and early-sixties and that was to serve as restricted housing for retired adults. Sometimes erected under the patronage of religious,

Fairly consistent with the garden apartment genre, regardless of style, is the growing use of individual balconies, which can also be found on new high-rise apartments, central air conditioning, and some special attempts at landscaping. Wood-burning fireplaces are also now featured. A design characteristic that becomes fairly common is the introduction of varying textures on the exterior through the use of several materials. There is an effort to introduce interesting silhouettes. Facades are enriched with projections, recessions, color and texture changes, all to avoid the monotony that can be easily a problem in large, multiple-unit designs, whether in an apartment building or a motel. Some of the garden apartments turned inward, as is the case of the apartments at 1111 W. 46th, called The Regent Apartments (Figs. 152 and 153). A 1965 design of Linscott, Kiene & Haylett, who also did The Mews, this apartment isolates itself from the congestion of the older residential section in which it was built by the use of the interior court while turning toward the streets curiously decorated solid walls topped with a clearstory. The sloping site provides for a constantly changing roof line that adds to the visual interest.

Fig. 153. COURTYARD OF THE REGENT APARTMENTS. (photo 1978)

Fig. 154. VISTA DEL RIO APARTMENTS, 600 Admiral. Completed in 1967, John L. Daw & Associates architects. (photo 1977)

professional or union organizations, these buildings do not vary very much from the norm for their general type. In fact, there were some remodelings for this purpose. However, care had to be taken to make sure that provision was made for people with the special interests and requirements of the elderly.

On occasion some handsome buildings were erected. One of the most interesting is the Vista Del Rio Apartments at 600 Admiral Boulevard (Fig. 154). A wide but not very deep high-rise of reinforced concrete and glass, which was designed by John L. Daw & Associates and completed in 1967, the exterior has a powerful composition that depends on the judicious use of small balconies and on the contrast of the light concrete with the darker glass areas. It is one of the most open, and most frankly expressed, of this genre of apartment building. It provides an interesting contrast to the Parkway Towers (Fig. 143). Built on urban renewal land, it is one of several structures in that area, but it is the most commanding in terms of its placement and bold facades. The extensive use of glass raises, of course, a variety of questions considering the fact that it was intended for residential use and for retired people. It was unlikely that this openness of exterior would attract very many imitators, although more conservative designs contemporary with it are not necessarily any more energy efficient. The Vista Del Rio is very much a product of its era, and we see few such light, open designs today. The style wheel has turned, at least in Kansas City, back toward a more hermetic design with more extensive masonry or concrete.

The development of new apartment buildings within the boundaries of the Kansas City, Missouri School District at this time might seem surprising given our comments on the matter of White Flight. While the new apartments were not restricted to White residents, they were so located that this would likely be the case for most. However, much of the new construction was meeting the housing needs of single adults, childless couples, and retired people, whose interest in schools was less personal. Some of these new facilities were, in fact, restricted to and intended to serve only these types of tenants. Within easy commuting distance of the central city's businesses and offices, and other major employers, such as the hospitals and medical centers, they also provided convenient access to cultural amenities and, quite important, to public transportation. The development of these new apartments represents one of the major architectural changes in the older residential areas north of 47th Street and west of Troost.

New apartments and new office buildings in Kansas City proper were not always located at the expense of older buildings, but as it turned out a good deal of them were. Repeating the patterns of earlier generations, the replacements of low density residences and shops with high density apartments and office buildings was seen as positive evidence of desirable growth. The remodeling and recycling of structures was also deemed desirable, and the major renovation of a warehouse into the Armed Forces Building at 2420 Broadway, in 1959, won a local AIA award for the architects, Geis, Hunter & Ramos (Fig. 155). It certainly gives no sign of ever being anything other than a new building of the late fifties. Along with the Macy's Store (Fig. 127), it was a persuasive argument for the benefits of this type of progressive design.

Fig. 155. ARMED FORCES BUILDING, 2420 Broadway. Remodeling project completed in 1959, Geis, Hunter & Ramos architects. (photo 1978)

138

Fig. 156. BMA (Business Men's Assurance Company) BUILDING, 700 W. 31st. Completed in 1964, Skidmore, Owings & Merrill architects. (photo 1978)

Concerns over the loss of older buildings and designs, if expressed at all, were muted, and the issues of historic preservation were not major public matters in this period.

Some commercial buildings in the sixties were noteworthy for their design, others for the way they also modified the cityscape. Possibly the most striking example of this is the Business Men's Assurance Building (Fig. 156), a product of the national firm of Skidmore, Owings & Merrill. It was erected away from the downtown, at the southwest corner of Penn Valley Park, a high point in the city's terrain. Completed in 1964, it is visible at a great distance, isolated from any significant competition for attention, other than a nearby television station tower. The BMA was not the first SOM building in Kansas City. Of its predecessors, one other was fairly large, the former John Hancock Building now Plaza Center just to the northwest of the Country Club Plaza, at 47th and Madison (Fig. 157). It was completed in 1963. Both SOM designs were novel for Kansas City, but they were not unique; there are stylistic siblings by SOM in other cities. The John Hancock's facades consist of precast, cruciform structural members that are placed to form a grid that is noticeably in front of the plane of the windows. Visual interest is carried primarily by the tapering of the vertical arms of the structural modules and their jointing together. The BMA repeats one concept, that of recessing the plane of the glass (the actual building envelope) well behind the exterior structural grid. On the BMA, this structural grid is

139

Fig. 157. PLAZA CENTER BUILDING (formerly JOHN HANCOCK BUILDING), 800 W. 47th. Completed in 1963, Skidmore, Owings & Merrill architects. (photo 1978)

140

Fig. 159. TENMAIN CENTER, northwest corner of Tenth and Main. Completed in 1968, Charles Luckman (Los Angeles) architect. (photo 1976)

Fig. 158. COMMERCE TOWER, 911 Main. Completed in 1965, Keene, Simpson & Murphy architects. (photo 1976)

clad in white marble, and the result is a crisp, elegantly rectangular pattern set off by the dark glass that lies behind it. With the same arrangement on all four facades (only the number of bays differ), the sky can be seen inside the corner columns, a subtle touch that animates what otherwise would be a uniform exterior treatment. At the ground level, the building is completely open except for a small entrance lobby. Situated by a park, poised on its rise of ground, set off by a simple plaza, the prize-winning building is one of the finest high-rise office towers ever erected in the city.

Downtown, the Commerce Bank erected a tall office building designed by Keene, Simpson & Murphy (Fig. 158), which was in operation in 1965. Located at Ninth and Main, the Commerce Tower was the first locally designed tall building since the completion of the City Hall. In contrast to the SOM buildings, the Commerce Tower presents a sheer facade, and though the structural grid is quite evident, it receives competition from the mullions that subdivide the glass of the envelope. With no columns at the outer corners,

there is a hint at a more complex exterior, but this potential was not exploited, perhaps due to an inherent conservatism, or as a concession to the austere geometry still favored in most design.

If we compare the several tall office towers built in this period, we can see that each was committed to a simple geometric shape. The Traders Bank, the first in the timeline, is the most cautious in design, but nevertheless a clear statement in a simple geometric vocabulary based on emphasizing structural elements. The BMA is, in many ways, the purest expression of the geometry of structure, since the outermost columns and girders stand beyond the surrounding walls of the building. Here, however, elegance of cladding material and special concern for proportions raise this design far above a mere expression of structure. The Commerce Bank continues in this vein, but now the division and subdivision of the facade—that includes both structure and building sheath—provides us with a more complex surface.

This building was followed by the TenMain Center, which

141

Fig. 160. MISSOURI DIVISION OF EMPLOYMENT SECURITY BUILDING, 1411 Main. View from the southwest. Construction started in 1966, Shaughnessy, Bower & Grimaldi architects. (photo 1978)

Fig. 161. MISSOURI DIVISION OF EMPLOYMENT SECURITY BUILDING, view from the southeast. (photo 1978)

142

was completed in 1968 (Fig. 159). Designed by Charles Luckman of Los Angeles, it continues the reliance on stark geometry. But now the exterior is clad in precast panels that create a noticeable texture through beveled openings and slight projections at horizontal joinings of the modules. It is more plastic in appearance than the other three, due to the variations of light and shade caused by its more complex surface. This foretold an important direction new architecture was to take, namely a return to a more sculptural quality in the design of the exterior of buildings, a retreat from the simple planes of the fifties and early sixties.

Another interesting example of this return of texture and plastic modeling to architectural design is the building for the Missouri Division of Employment Security at 1411 Main (Figs. 160 and 161). A four-level building designed by Shaughnessy, Bower & Grimaldi, the exterior is dominated by bold shapes with the walls executed in buff, textured concrete. Construction began in 1966. The tense, bold patterning and textures provide a sharp contrast to the quiet equilibrium of the Armed Forces Building (Fig. 155), which was completed less than a decade earlier and is about the same size. The Missouri building is one of a number of structures designed in the second half of the sixties that usher in, in Kansas City, a new architectural esthetic, which is more concerned with pronounced, cast shadows and contrasting textures, than with color and planar subdivisions to animate the exterior. The building for the Missouri Division of Employment Security is also one of a number of government-service buildings built at this time. Another, which shows a somewhat different path away from severe geometrics, is the new Federal Office Building.

The Federal Building (Figs. 162 and 163) was the work of Associated Architects and Engineers of Kansas City, a consortium of local architects: Voskamp & Slezak; Everett & Keleti; and Radotinsky, Meyn & Deardorff, with Harris Armstrong of St. Louis consulting, and Howard, Needles, Tammen & Bergendoff structural engineers. Located on the two square blocks due east of the Jackson County Courthouse, from Locust to Holmes, and from Twelfth to Thirteenth, the design was completed in late 1962 and the

building was occupied in 1966. The eighteen-story building is the largest office building in the city. Basically it consists of a large, thin slab oriented east and west and a low projecting wing on the north side. The north and south facades are clad with metal panels that include windows and set up an alternating rhythm that is repeated, offset, at the spandrel level. The resulting effect is a checkered pattern that reads as a texture on the huge facades. The lateral exterior walls each

Fig. 162. Portion of south facade of the FEDERAL OFFICE BUILDING with the JACKSON COUNTY COURTHOUSE. (photo 1972)

Fig. 163. FEDERAL OFFICE BUILDING, 601 E. Twelfth. View from the northwest. Designed in 1966, Voskamp & Slezak, Everett & Keleti, Radotinsky, Meyn & Deardorff, with Harris Armstrong (St. Louis) consulting architects; Howard, Needles, Tammen & Bergendoff structural engineers. (photo 1977)

consist of two blank panels of stone that are offset at a slight angle and are separated from each other (See Fig. 165). The horizontal bulk of the building, extending as it does through two blocks, gives one the illusion that the pattern on the facade is quite small. The building is also a strong contrast to the verticality and the style of the County Courthouse and the City Hall, its immediate neighbors.

To the south of the Federal Building is the much smaller Missouri State Building, a design of Kivett & Myers which was completed in 1968 (Fig. 164). Despite its much smaller size and different style from that of its large companion, it relates far better to the Federal Building than does either the City Hall or the Courthouse. The State Building is set so far back from the giant to the north that the plaza which fronts it and covers a parking garage, is nearly a full city block square. It, too, like the Federal Building, is a horizontal structure. Similarly, the facade depends on a regular rectangular repetition of windows, which in this case are in precast modules analogous to those used on the TenMain Center

Fig. 164. MISSOURI STATE BUILDING, 615 E. Thirteenth. Completed in 1968, Kivett & Myers architects. (photo 1977)

(Fig. 159) and with the same result.

Though not apparent in the view shown in Figure 164, the plaza that fronts the State Building is flanked at a lower level on the east by St. Mary's Episcopal Church (Fig. 48). There is less visual conflict between these two buildings than one might expect, even though they are so different in function, age and style. First, there is a relationship in the matter of scale and austerity of design, and second, being placed offset and at right angles to one another, the discrepancies are less manifest. This arrangement, however, does not set up another implied "quadrangle" of the sort discussed in conjunction with the 1930s civic center. The placement of the two new government buildings, for federal and state needs, to the east and southeast of the city and county buildings, neither extends nor complements the earlier civic plan. When one adds the visual weight of the new library building to the west (Fig. 142), one finds about eight square blocks devoted to public buildings, a large area that lacks a dominant visual focus or an integrating design (Fig. 165). This deficiency may not bother some people, but it should. Part of the reason for placing these buildings near each other and downtown was to help the heart of the city survive and to serve as a model for what enlightened urban renewal could do to revitalize a city. No one person, firm or agency is to be blamed for the failure, for the same evidence of lost opportunities can be found in every city and on every college campus. It takes strong and enlightened leadership as well as extraordinarily talented design to accomplish effective city planning over a long period and a large area. These traits tend to conflict with taste arrived at through consensual democracy, and with vested property rights which some want to place above all else.

As an architectural addendum to the area's new architecture, there is one other building that should be mentioned. This is the new Greyhound Bus Terminal (Fig. 166) that was constructed to the northeast of the Federal Building. The Kivett & Myers design at Twelfth and Holmes was under construction in 1966. A low-lying building that covers the entire block, it is more in harmony with the State Building than the Federal Building diagonally across the street. Its design is simple, using structural members for principal

144

Fig. 165. View of CIVIC CENTER from the southwest. From left to right: CITY HALL; PUBLIC LIBRARY; MUNICIPAL COURTS BUILDING (partially visible); JACKSON COUNTY COURTHOUSE; and FEDERAL OFFICE BUILDING. (photo 1978)

Fig. 166. GREYHOUND BUS TERMINAL, Eleventh to Twelfth, Holmes to Charlotte. Constructed in 1966, Kivett & Myers architects. (photo 1977)

146

features in the form of paired columns punctuating the long horizontal exterior. Parking is carried on the roof over the waiting and ticketing room, and the adjacent freight, garage and platform areas. The simple design provides a utilitarian building that is also visually interesting in its own right, though in its isolation at the edge of the central business district it does seem a bit lost.

Regardless of what one might think of individual designs or of their placement in the city, there can be no question but that a lot of construction was underway in the 1960s, including the freeway system which celebrated the completion of Interstate 70, in Missouri, in 1962. Architecturally, the city was very much alive and this stimulated new plans. In December of 1966, Kansas City voters approved a $150 million revenue bond package for the new airport, then called Mid-Continent International Airport, with the expectation of the new facility opening in 1970.

In June, 1967, a Jackson County capital improvements bond issue, the first such in thirty years was approved. This was for somewhat more than $102,385,000, with forty-three million designated for a sports complex to house the baseball and football teams, and fourteen million designated for a new

general hospital. In a very brief period the voters had approved a quarter of a billion dollars in bonds that represented some massive construction projects.

These were joined by an even more remarkable venture, namely the announced plans for a city within a city, a $115 million residential and business community to be created by private funds within the area between Hospital Hill and Liberty Memorial, just to the southeast of the Union Station.

Sponsored by Hallmark Cards Incorporated, whose new office building (Fig. 138) and warehouse were located in the area, the Crown Center project was a long-range plan to transform an area that consisted primarily of industrial and commercial structures into an ultra-modern, people-oriented center. Basic to the success of this plan was the early erection of a group of office buildings to be followed by a large deluxe-class hotel, and a quality retail shopping center. Underlying the entire complex, was to be extensive inside parking for thousands of automobiles. Apartments and condominium buildings were scheduled to be added later, along with other offices and appropriate businesses. In totality, the plan was extraordinarily ambitious, and if completed as visualized, it could rival and possibly displace the central business district as the heart of the city.

Elsewhere in the city, additional construction was taking place. At the University several major buildings were under construction following a merger in 1963 that made the school the western urban campus of the University of Missouri. This solved the immediate financial crisis of the old University of Kansas City, along with the pressure for low-cost university education in the Kansas City area. One of these was a new, general library building that was opened in 1968 (Fig. 167). This was the earliest incontestable evidence of the changes wrought by the affiliation of the University of Kansas City with the venerable State University, for the library was the first large-scale structure completed on the Volker Campus. A design of Marshall & Brown, the library is a fine example of the trait that was developing in architecture at that time, namely the introduction of a more constructivist approach to design, along with a heavier, more robust look (compare with Fig. 142). In the case of the library building,

Fig. 167. GENERAL LIBRARY, Volker Campus, University of Missouri-Kansas City. Completed in 1968, Marshall & Brown architects. (photo 1978)

the scale of the individual components, such as the projecting segments of the facade are not ponderous. There is a gracefulness that serves the library quite well. When analyzed, one can see how simple the basic concept is, but also how subtly proportioned it is in scale and details.

The activity on the construction front in 1968 was quite possibly the most significant seen in the city, which had witnessed other concerted bursts of building, in 1888, in 1906, and in 1929-30. But there were some negative portents. There was the construction strike in 1967 which lasted ten weeks. Each building craft negotiated its own contract, and these did not expire at the same time, creating the potential of sequential strikes, which did occur in 1969 and 1970. Strikes were avoided in 1968, but in that year the city was wracked by the riots that followed the assassination of Dr. Martin Luther King. Significant damage was done in sections of the inner city. That year also saw the closing of a landmark retail store, Emery, Bird, Thayer (Fig. 46), and the demolition of the second Board of Trade Building (Fig. 43).

Then, in 1969, the city was hit by the first of what turned out to be two lengthy construction strikes. This first one was of four months duration. It was followed by the strike of 1970 that lasted 201 days. When that one started, it was estimated that in the metropolitan area, there was nearly three billion dollars of current or planned construction underway that was affected. In 1969 the city had led the nation in man-days lost to strikes of all kinds. The following year was more devastating in time lost. Within four years, from 1967 through 1970, over one calendar year had been lost to major construction, and every important architectural project in the city was affected.

When construction resumed in late 1970, things once again seemed extraordinarily busy, but in fact the great construction boom of the late 1960s had peaked. The labor instability exhibited in the Kansas City area, when coupled with rising costs, began to reduce the rate at which investments in architecture occurred. Things did not slow down abruptly, of course, but there was a slowdown and a cooling of enthusiasm which had managed to gain passage for a quarter of a billion dollars in public capital improvements. Grand plans were still being outlined. Construction was underway, and demolition in anticipation of new buildings, or to ease tax losses on empty buildings, went forward. This was mostly on momentum generated by government appropriations and bond monies that were finite and not likely to be replenished in like amounts in the 1970s.

In 1970, the city's area was 316 square miles in three counties, with the final annexation having become effective in January, 1963. The city's population was counted as 507,000. In 1950, the city's population, which was residing in about 20% of the 1970 area, was nearly 457,000. A decade earlier, in nearly the same area, the population was 399,000. Obviously, the older core of the city had not increased in population since 1950, and in fact there had been a decline. What growth had occurred had taken place in the annexed areas, beyond the Kansas City School District. But an even more substantial growth had occurred in the suburbs, particularly in Johnson County, Kansas. Add to this demographic situation the reconstitution of traffic patterns in the area and

147

one can easily demonstrate that by 1970 Kansas City had become a very different place from the city which had greeted the end of World War II. Kansas City had, in fact, become the place-name that designated a large metropolitan area covering large sections of five counties in two states, as well as the name for the city that had grown from Chouteau's landing. The name also designated a media market of a million and a quarter people in seven counties, rather than something less than half that number in the city proper. Kansas City had become a place where "downtown" carried little meaning for the majority of the region's residents. In fact, it had become irrelevant as a place for more and more people. The city had evolved into a sprawling area that depended on the automobile first, and looked to the airport rather than the railroad station as the alternative to private transportation.

Large sections of the older city were neglected and even gutted. New residential development turned to self-contained shopping centers—of which more than seventy had been created in the metropolitan area since 1950—as the place to shop, transact business, and seek services. The replacement construction that was built in the older city was in response to the convenience inherent in a converging freeway system more than to the economic advantages that would accrue by concentrating the business of government, banking and industry within close proximity of each other.

Somewhere in the 1960s, the city which had evolved between the end of the Civil War and the start of World War II had begun to wither. Conceptually and physically it was being replaced by a new urban mass, a conglomerate of parts that seemed to need and yet not want direction from, nor the benefits of a dominant central core. The Kansas City of Van Brunt and Howe was being rapidly erased. The Kansas City of Louis Curtiss and John McKecknie was expendable. Soon perhaps that of Wight & Wight, and Hoit, Price & Barnes, would be vulnerable. The new architecture being built could not hide the fact that in the older city more and more one could find empty buildings and empty lots. The constant refurbishing of the Country Club Plaza kept it alive and attractive. Elsewhere the intersection-based business districts were being displaced by the self-contained shopping center. The surge of building that had been interrupted by the two great strikes had been designed with the awareness that the results were dependent on automobile commuters, people who might live considerable distances from these facilities. Most of these people did not want nor intend to use public transportation if they could help it, or deal on a daily basis with the problems of the aging, inner city.

By 1970, the residents of Kansas City and its suburbs had turned away from the urban values—and thus the city—of the past. Yet there was one continuing dream, a little less vivid now, that Kansas City would someday become the Metropolis of the Midlands. This was no longer the nineteenth century conception of a metropolis, but rather the new version which saw a great metropolitan area tied together by a network of expressways. Located within this area was the older city, but this was visibly changing and in places even disappearing. The enormous changes and increasing losses had finally begun to concern more than a few people, people who lived in the suburbs as well as people who lived in the older city. More and more people were questioning the concept that progress could be measured best by the size and the newness of things, or that new growth inevitably had to be at the expense of the old.

In 1970, as the city endured its second consecutive construction season with a massive work stoppage, there was time to assess the losses of architecture that had occurred with no replacements planned, or pending, or likely now to be feasible. Finally, a countermovement was launched, and a perceptible change began to take place within the metropolitan area. In a halting way, one period was ending for the city, and another was beginning.

1970-1976
Progress Plus Preservation

When the long strike of 1970 ended, architectural progress was so far behind schedule that the early years of the decade were marked by the completion of projects long overdue, that had been expected to cap the building surge of the 1960s. This time-slippage was not the only effect. Planning now had to take into account increased costs and a history of labor instability that had shut down construction for three lengthy periods in four years. The adjustments in attitudes that attended these changes were subtle and their impact was only gradually felt. A parallel situation of quiet change was also occurring in the field of architectural preservation.

Historic preservation in both the city and the county had begun to gather strength in the 1960s, and none too soon if the tide of demolition and decay that was affecting the older city was to be stemmed. What modest support could be provided by the National Historic Preservation Act of 1966 was welcome. Losses had been mounting, despite some local efforts to save and maintain historic property. An important early source for positive action was the revitalized Jackson County Historical Society. The Historical Society had turned to some architectural preservation problems in the late 1950s. With major support for the Society coming from the Independence area, it is not surprising that the earliest preservation success of the Society was the purchase and renovation of the antebellum Old Jail and Marshall's House in Independence, which were made into museum structures.

Soon thereafter, in 1962, the Society supported planning for a county project to create a museum village from relocated structures, thereby saving them from demolition. Called Missouri Town 1855, and located in eastern Jackson County, it has proven to be a success, though its purpose and character did not lend itself to the preservation of Kansas City's buildings. Nevertheless, a favorable climate for preservation was being established. The now experienced Historical Society acquired the Wornall Residence (Figs. 12 and 13) in 1964 with the intent of restoring it to its original 1858 appearance and maintaining it as a museum house on its original site. This project, too, has been successful. In fact, the Wornall Residence became the first Kansas City structure to be entered on the National Register of Historic Places, in 1969.

Notable as these accomplishments were, they could hardly offset the large-scale demolitions that concurrently were taking place. Yet, these successes encouraged other groups to accept other challenges. One of these was the drive to preserve St. Mary's Episcopal Church (Fig. 48), which had been isolated on a terrain that had been stripped bare to receive the new federal and state office buildings. St. Mary's was saved in 1964 through the efforts of loyal parishioners and some timely gifts, despite the belief by many that it had outlived its usefulness and would be an anomaly in a non-residential area. Granted, today it operates somewhat differently than when it had been built, but its continuance is now well accepted, and its status is secure.

As part of this growing local involvement in historic architecture, a Missouri Valley Chapter of the Society of

Architectural Historians was formed in 1966, with principal activities headquartered in the city. While the SAH is more a learned society than an activist agency, preservation concerns were an important contributing factor to the establishment of the chapter. For a growing number of people, it was becoming all too clear that ongoing and organized group action was needed to voice alternatives to demolition, alternatives that would be listened to and hopefully heeded. Despite the existence of organizations, and the evidence of some successes, the preservation movement in the area was not very powerful and its energies were aimed in several directions. It was also then trying to operate without the important assistance of a local landmarks law that could apply to specific cases. Thus, when the Board of Trade Building (Figs. 43 and 44) was scheduled for demolition in 1968, it turned out that there was little that concerned people could do beyond pointing out the enormity of the pending loss, and to search without success for a way to save it. But people were now conscious of the fact that a building of importance was threatened and that its loss was irremediable. A short inventory of historic buildings in the metropolitan area was made soon thereafter by a committee of the Kansas City Chapter of the American Institute of Architects. While modest in scope, this survey was a step of considerable importance because it provided a specific professional response to the demolitions related to urban redevelopment. In the accompanying exhibit, losses were illustrated as well as historic buildings still standing. This inventory also became the point of departure for a more thoroughly researched survey which the Landmarks Commission undertook soon after its formation.

The creation of a Landmarks Commission of the City of Kansas City, Missouri in 1970 was one of the most significant steps taken in the city in the attempt to cope with the growing crisis in the documentation and preservation of historically important buildings. Though the ordinance that created the commission also limited quite severely its powers, the fact that a Landmarks Commission with a budget was established indicated that there was now an understanding that preservation was indeed an issue in which the public

had an interest, an interest that should be represented through a city commission. And it did not take long for a case to arise that demonstrated the importance of this.

On June 30, 1971, a tentative plan was announced for the transformation of the land holdings of the Kansas City Terminal Railway Company in the immediate area of the Union Station (Fig. 81) into a large complex of high-rise apartments and office buildings, with a central shopping plaza, transportation facilities and parking areas. The plan rather obviously avoided mention of the great terminal building, and thus one could presume that it was to be demolished. The rapid decline of passenger train service during the 1960s had eliminated the necessity for the vast waiting room and numerous passenger platforms, and the substitution of air and truck for rail transport in the movement of the mail had further reduced the need for the vast lower reaches of the terminal. The Union Station, in the sixty years since Jarvis Hunt had completed its design, had become completely obsolete as a railroad terminal.

As early as March of 1968 there had been some preliminary discussions on alternative uses for the station, with mention of its possible use by the Kansas City Museum, but this was simply talk. By 1971, the Union Station was seriously threatened, and unless something could be done it was doomed to demolition. The Landmarks Commission, though still in its organizational period, had a sizable issue confronting it and a pressing task to do. In many ways it was the Union Station crisis, and the involvement of the new Landmarks Commission and other groups in the struggle to save the station, that marks the beginning of a major preservation movement in Kansas City.

The task of saving and recycling the station has not been easy to resolve, and though the threat of demolition now seems remote, as of this writing one cannot report that the building is, in fact, secure. However, after a great many hours of effort and planning by many people, it does seem very promising that the science and technology portion of the Kansas City Museum will be relocated in the great lobby and the lower floors of the headhouse, while offices of the Internal Revenue Service will be housed in the upper levels of

Fig. 168. KCI (KANSAS CITY INTERNATIONAL) AIRPORT, parking and entrance areas for Terminal Building C, with the Airport Tower in the distance. Completed in 1972, Kivett & Myers architects. (photo 1978)

the station. Also being planned nearby is a large IRS facility that will be on land that once was covered with train sheds. How the new architecture will relate to the old is not yet certain. One can hope that there will be a concern for an effective intermingling of the two.

Because of the long strikes in the construction industry in 1969 and 1970, the first major buildings of the seventies were completions of structures designed and started before 1969, and there was a sequence of important openings from 1971 to 1973. The long hiatus—for all practical purposes lasting two years—marks these delayed projects not only as a culmination of the great building boom of the mid-sixties, but also as part of the context within which preservation issues and cases were being argued and judged. Among the building projects which had stood idle during the extended months of the strike were two that represented popular public programs. These were the new airport facilities, and the new sports complex, each a multi-building project.

The new airport, now called Kansas City International

Airport (KCI), officially replaced Municipal Airport as the commercial air passenger terminal in November, 1972. The principal buildings, in addition to various service structures, were designed by Kivett & Myers and consisted of three identical terminal structures with room for a fourth, and a control tower and administration building. The site is so vast and, except for the tower, so low-lying, that it is virtually impossible to comprehend the layout from a ground-level view. What one sees from the air are three, almost closed circles—the terminals—centered sixty degrees apart around half of the circumference of a larger circle. Within the latter is located the tower and administration building. The terminal buildings ring parking lots. Additional parking is located in several lots within the large central circle. The entire complex is linked with roads that follow the dominant circular plan. The multiple terminals and circular patterning resulted from a desire to gain the maximum of terminal space for aircraft while reducing the distance a passenger would have to walk from a terminal entrance to a loading gate.

The entire facility is constructed of buff reinforced concrete that also serves as the principal surface finish of both the interior and the exterior (Figs. 168, 169 and 170). The way poured concrete is used to form both structure and massive building shapes, with resulting bold patterns of light and shade, is hardly unique to this complex. There are ample precedents for this in twentieth century architecture. Locally there are a few examples, but nothing so large and so blunt, inside and out, as these terminals. Rising costs in labor and materials, already a factor in the sixties, forced architects to give serious consideration to the economic advantages of having structural members made of reinforced concrete and then allowing this material to stand as the final finish. Concrete came out, so to speak, from behind the veneer. As revealed, concrete became a building finish and so the plasticity inherent in the material was exploited to produce bold shapes and textures. These were grouped with an eye to sculptural qualities as well as architectonic function. One recalls a similar treatment in the Missouri Division of Employment Security building (Figs. 160 and 161).

The special architectural problems generated by large

151

Fig. 169. KCI AIRPORT, interior of Terminal Building C, by Gate 65 (Ozark Airlines). (photo 1978)

commercial airports in the United States include the provision for direct gate-access to a large number of aircraft, and the need to accommodate a number of separate airline companies, each with its own identifiable area. One response to these problems is to decentralize terminal facilities as at KCI. Busy airports also generate a considerable amount of bus and automobile traffic, bringing employees, passengers and visitors to and from the facility. With the high dependence on private automobiles that exists in the Kansas City area, large amounts of convenient parking became another requirement at KCI. If we add the desire to provide private automobile access directly at the terminals, and placing terminal entrances near loading gates, the configuration for the complex we've already noted becomes almost inevitable. Each C-shaped terminal is comparatively narrow in cross-section (Fig. 169). Each has numerous entrances, permitting arriving passengers to enter the terminal at or very near the departure gate. Correspondingly, after arrival and baggage claim, one of the many terminal exits is near at hand.

Each terminal is built on two levels (Fig. 170), though the

Fig. 170. KCI AIRPORT, aircraft side of Terminal Building B, with portion of Terminal Building C in the foreground. (photo 1978)

passengers use only the upper one. Parking within the circle created by a terminal is set below the entrance-level of the building, and so a clear vista is provided (See Fig. 168.). The terminal exteriors are austere, and one might even say elegant if simple in shape, proportions and detail. At ground-level, while arriving or departing, or transferring from one terminal to another, the low-lying, curving shapes constantly change in relationship to each other. Yet they always seem to be a basic set which is anchored by the vertical rectilinearity of the control tower at the central focus of the entire complex.

Inside the terminals, the curved space truncates one's view of what otherwise would be a vista of little change insofar as detailing is concerned. In fact, the vastness is so well concealed it is only when one is required to go from one gate to another, or from one terminal to another, that one senses the largeness of the building. Interior ornament, other than that provided by the airlines to identify their areas, is limited to the functional wood panels that are used to isolate boarding lounges and form various enclosures, and to the revealed structural units that create interesting shapes and patterns.

Something of this same scale and directness of expression can be found at the Truman Sports Complex which is located near the interchange of Interstate 435 with Interstate 70. At that location, two stadiums were built, one for football and the other for baseball, both designed by Kivett & Myers (Fig. 171). The sports complex is more readily comprehended at ground level than is the airport, since the two stadiums are close to each other and aligned on axis. The great size of the enterprise is immediately apparent, and it is impressively big. As with the new airport, which was overbuilt to meet anticipated future needs, here it was argued that a single, multi-purpose stadium would be less effective for a given sport. On the premise that games would not be scheduled concurrently, support facilities, most notably parking lots and access roads, could be shared.

Initially, a movable arched roof that could track from one to the other was to be shared hence the axial alignment—but its cost became prohibitive and it was abandoned. At each

153

154

Fig. 171. TRUMAN SPORTS COMPLEX. Arrowhead Stadium (left) completed in 1972, and Royals Stadium completed in 1973, Kivett & Myers architects. (photo 1978)

stadium, a principal design determinant was the intention to place an optimum number of people in comfortable seats as close to the playing field as possible. This functional factor, plus others, such as the provision for quick and easy access and egress for tens of thousands of people, and the provision for night-game illumination, determined the shapes of the architecture. Sweeping, curved shapes in reinforced concrete are the result. These shapes are the dominant characteristic of the two dissimilar yet closely related stadiums (Fig. 172).

Without having to compromise to meet multi-purpose needs, there are no contradictions in the organization of space or its utilization. Each facility's design is rooted in the interaction between the prescribed playing field, the optimum number of seats, and the necessary service and support elements that each sport requires. In many ways the stadiums are pure examples of form following function, even more so than at the airport. Arrowhead Stadium for football was the first completed, in fall, 1972. In spring, 1973, Royals Stadium for baseball was ready for use.

The stadiums, which were funded by county bonds, are placed in the eastern section of Kansas City, quite close to Independence and to Raytown. When a new stadium for the city was first mooted, one location that was actively supported was the area to the south of the Municipal Auditorium, on the other side of the crosstown section of the downtown freeway loop. But as the project grew in size, the political practicalities of locating a county-funded facility were considered. A more central site in the county was demonstrated to be more practicable, and the large areas that had to be given to parking were more readily provided. The location near the intersection of two freeways also made access convenient from Johnson County in Kansas, and from north of the river.

The advantages or disadvantages of placing a stadium in the heart of the older city can be argued to no conclusion. At best, even a multi-purpose stadium is unlikely to be sched-

Fig. 172. RAMPS AT ROYALS STADIUM, Truman Sports Complex. (photo 1978)

uled by the principal tenants for more than a quarter of the year, and special events are not likely to add many more days. Yet, it would bring people into the downtown area at night and on weekends as do other entertainment facilities. But since no single category of activity makes or breaks a vital urban center, Kansas City's downtown depends on more than a rejuvenation of the entertainment industry, or the hotel and convention business, or the number of people employed by government and financial institutions within the downtown freeway loop, though collectively these are important. To avoid total obsolescence as a focus for the entire urban community, downtown must create and maintain a healthy round-the-clock and round-the-week mix of activities and peoples. This task is complex and demanding. It is not solved by any one project or program. This can be seen at what is really a textbook example of planning a multi-function urban center—Crown Center (Fig. 178).

Crown Center is a large-scale redevelopment project that has been underway since 1968, with completion anticipated in the late 1980s. The principal backer has been Hallmark Cards Incorporated, whose headquarters building (Fig. 138) and adjacent warehouse have become the initial elements in the comprehensive plan to redevelop completely a 25-block area between Liberty Memorial and Hospital Hill, from Main to Gillham Road, from 22nd Street to 27th Terrace. Prior to 1968, except for the two Hallmark structures, the area was a conglomerate of largely nondescript buildings set off by Signboard Hill, an unsightly remnant after the Main Street cut had been completed through the hill south of the Union Station, in 1912.

Enlightened self-interest, coupled with a concern for the older city, led Hallmark officials to concern themselves with the environment in which they and their employees worked. Rather than abandon the inner city, a revitalization was visualized. A redevelopment project for the area was announced in January 1967. Upgrading of existing buildings alone would not suffice though this was done with the Hallmark warehouse. Rather, there was an intention to create a completely new setting, one that would include, beside the Hallmark structures, a hotel, office buildings, retail

155

Fig. 173. CROWN CENTER OFFICE BUILDINGS, Pershing Road facades from the southeast. Completed in 1971, Edward Larrabee Barnes (New York) architect. (photo 1978)

156

shops and residential structures.

Victor Gruen & Associates of Los Angeles, and Larry Smith & Company of Seattle were selected to do the preliminary planning. The first plans called for a $115 million complex, that has since been expanded to nearly $400 million. Present plans call for the completion of some fifty buildings, including two million square feet of office space, two retail complexes, two hotels and various cultural and entertainment facilities.

Construction on the massive project began in September 1968, and the initial work concentrated on an enormous excavation that reduced much of Signboard Hill and opened up a sizable area east of Main and south of Pershing Road. This was to provide for: the substructure for five interlocking office buildings (Fig. 173) north of the Hallmark offices; a large hotel (Fig. 175) on Pershing Road between Grand and Main; and a vast, multi-level parking garage. When Crown Center is completed, there will be sheltered parking for some 5,000 automobiles, a sizable investment in itself.

As with the airport and the sports complex, Crown Center

was delayed by the construction strikes. It was not until late in 1971 that the five office buildings were opened. Designed by Edward Larrabee Barnes (New York), the coordinating architect for Crown Center, with Marshall & Brown associated, these essentially identical structures, each with its own entrance, elevators, etc., are linked in a zig-zag that ascends up the curve of Pershing Road as it swings from east to south below Hospital Hill. From the east (Fig. 173), they present a series of geometrically conceived blocks, each fronting on a lawn and circular drive. From the west, they stand almost as if they were massive city walls enclosing a large, terraced plaza area (Fig. 174). The entire arrangement consists of interconnected, rectangular shapes and volumes, all tightly defined in light grey, precast panels. A Barnes-designed banking facility brings the group over to Grand, completing the enclosure on the north of the plaza.

The impressive concept of Crown Center has never been in question, but it was not until the hotel and the retail shops opened, respectively in the spring and fall of 1973, that the general public became involved and caught up in the actuality of Crown Center. The hotel (Figs. 175 and 176) was designed by Harry Weese of Chicago. It presents a crisp and

Fig. 174. CROWN CENTER OFFICE BUILDINGS and CROWN CENTER SQUARE from the west. (photo 1979)

Fig. 175. CROWN CENTER HOTEL, from the northwest. Opened in 1973, Harry Weese & Associates (Chicago) architects. (photo 1973)

Fig. 176. CROWN CENTER HOTEL, from the northeast. RETAIL SHOPS, and SAN FRANCISCO TOWER to the left. (photo 1978)

Fig. 177. CROWN CENTER HOTEL, upper lobby, hillside garden. (photo 1978)

158

somewhat formidable, two-part exterior arrangement, which is best seen from the west (Fig. 175). The multi-level lobby and function building extends at street-level toward Pershing and Grand. Atop the former Signboard Hill is the L-shaped guest structure with over 700 rooms. Together, they represent a twenty-story elevation. Enclosed between these two units, utilizing the stone face of the hill, a terraced garden largely under glass (Fig. 177) provides a dramatic transitional space that is unique to the city, and has few parallels elsewhere. This exciting, almost Baroque spatial experience, has become a major tourist attraction in the city. It has contributed to the flow of people to and through Crown Center, a flow needed to complete the concept intended by the redevelopment to create a gathering, working, and living place for people.

Another element in developing a people-magnet, was the design and construction of the retail and restaurant space along Grand, immediately south of the convention portion of the hotel. This, too, was designed by Barnes, with Charles J. Breyer of New York doing the interior planning (Figs. 176 and 178). Across Grand Avenue is an open space backed by the rising terraces leading to the office buildings (Figs. 174 and 178). This plaza, called Crown Center Square, has become during most of the year a center of entertainments, ranging from ethnic fairs to craft shows to musical performances. Thus Crown Center Square also attracts large numbers of people, particularly on the weekends and evenings. In keeping with the public square idea, much in the manner of the Plaza at Rockefeller Center in New York, Crown Center Square has become the site for the annual Mayor's Christmas Tree display. It also has, on an adjacent terrace, a cold-weather ice skating rink.

The success of the initial buildings and Crown Center Square set the stage for the construction of the first residential units which were completed in 1976 (Fig. 179). This phase of construction included an apartment block of 110 units called Santa Fe Place, and a 32-story condominium unit called San Francisco Tower. These stylistically linked structures, with sheltered parking, tennis courts and other amenities, are due south of the retail block and are a design of The

Fig. 178. MODEL OF CROWN CENTER with existing and planned structures. (photo 1978)

160

Fig. 179. SAN FRANCISCO TOWER with SANTA FE APARTMENTS to the left. Completed in 1976, The Architects Collaborative (Cambridge, Mass.) architects. View of CROWN CENTER from the south, looking down Grand Avenue. (photo 1978)

Architects Collaborative of Cambridge, Massachusetts. Norman Fletcher is the principal involved. They did not repeat the style of the earlier structures, and some color was introduced, but the residential units relate quite well to the other buildings, for they were anticipated in the initial planning for the entire complex.

The impact, visual and social, of the transformation of the area south of Pershing Road along Grand Avenue was enormous. An early effect was the decision to build a high-rise office building of twenty-seven stories with a four-story satellite. Located due north of the 1971 office buildings across Pershing Road, the Mutual Benefit Life Building and adjacent IBM Plaza were announced in 1975. The buildings, designed by the office of Mies van der Rohe of Chicago, were completed in 1977 (Fig. 180). These are in a slightly retardataire style, harking back to the taste and design of the 1960s, but the tower still works well as an important component of the complex. The structural members are made of reinforced concrete, but these are completely concealed behind a cladding of anodized aluminum and double-glazed solar glass.

Early in 1978, excavations began for a 45-story Hyatt Regency hotel to be built immediately northeast of the MBL tower. This is being designed by a consortium of local architects. With that announcement, and envisioning the future plans for Crown Center, it is clear that Crown Center can become a serious competitor to downtown for its historic role as the business, hotel and convention center of the city. In what manner coordination or competition between these two locales will occur or be resolved is uncertain. There is also the possibility that Grand Avenue could become an important and exciting strip of quality buildings linking the two centers and thus enhancing the development of both.

One of the attractive features of Crown Center is the density and the visual interaction of a group of buildings that provide various pedestrian levels, interesting spaces and vistas. This has come about because there has been a carefully reasoned plan for development. An important component in this has been the placement of a large portion of the parking in multi-level structures which have a sophisticated security system. Almost totally enclosed, parking

Fig. 180. MUTUAL BENEFIT LIFE INSURANCE COMPANY BUILDING and IBM PLAZA at CROWN CENTER. Completed in 1977, office of Mies van der Rohe architects. (photo 1978)

161

does not compete visually with the structures intended to shelter people. Admittedly expensive, ranging from $3,000 per space for rented office parking, to $8,000 per space for the apartments, this provision has enabled the architects to avoid the gap-toothed appearance that surface lots produce in so much of downtown—the type of parking that denotes demolished buildings rather than planned development. This is not the place to argue either the economic or cultural issues implicit in this practice. Rather, the point is that Crown Center represents a different approach than that used in the downtown area to deal with the task of accommodating the automobile, though we must recognize that there are some surface lots in the Crown Center area. We might add that an attitude similar to that which prevails at Crown Center, of providing the automobile with extensive sheltered parking, has been a feature for years at the Country Club Plaza. This has helped it to compete successfully with the newer shopping malls.

Fig. 181. H. ROE BARTLE EXHIBITION HALL, Twelfth to Fourteenth, Central to Broadway. View from the northeast. Opened in 1976, Seligson Associates, Inc., Horner & Blessing, C. F. Murphy & Associates (Chicago) architects, and Howard, Needles, Tammen & Bergendoff structural engineers. (photo 1978)

162

Fig. 182. View in exhibition area of BARTLE HALL. (photo 1978)

Of course we must acknowledge that in contrast to both Crown Center and the Country Club Plaza, downtown has to cope with multitudinous ownerships of property, and the competing priorities that prevail there. But downtown also presents a problem not found at the Crown Center location. That is the presence of viable, older buildings that have much to offer, and which should be retained, and are interspersed within a development area that will receive new construction. New buildings are needed downtown not only to replace inadequate or deteriorated structures, but also to meet needs which are beyond the capabilities or capacities of the existing building stock. This does provide a challenge that has been avoided at Crown Center.

Two needs of this sort, which various people early had identified as requiring new construction downtown, were a very large exhibition facility, and another large first-class hotel, both in the immediate vicinity of Municipal Auditorium. The argument was that both were needed if Kansas City was to compete successfully for large conventions, an important source of sustenance for the downtown of a city once it had lost its historic role as the principal retail center. The benefits to downtown, it was argued, would prove to be assets for the larger community. So after some eight years of talk and some halting starts, and after a very close vote, the first of these needs was realized when the H. Roe Bartle Exhibition Hall was funded, and then finally opened late in 1976 (Fig. 181).

Bartle Hall, covering two full blocks, is adjacent to the Municipal Auditorium. Gaining bond approval for the $38 million project had been difficult, but the effort led to the construction of an enormous structure that contains about 435,000 square feet of usable space, of which nearly half is clear-span exhibition space. It was designed by a four-company team: Seligson Associates, Inc.; Horner & Blessing; C. F. Murphy & Associates of Chicago; and Howard, Needles, Tammen & Bergendoff. The building is noteworthy for its award-winning engineering of the clear-span exhibition space, using an adaptation of bridge-type trusses, forty-eight in all, each spanning 303 feet (Fig. 182). The awesome bulk is impressive. For that reason it is an awkward companion to

Fig. 183. R. CROSBY KEMPER MEMORIAL ARENA, 1800 Genesee. Completed in 1976, C. F. Murphy & Associates (Chicago) architects. View from the east. (photo 1978)

the Municipal Auditorium (Fig. 114) to which it is connected by underground passage. Bartle Hall did what earlier seemed impossible. It reduced the monolithic massiveness of the Municipal Auditorium, and now the mid-thirties building actually appears to be a richly decorated building when its fine stonework and sculptured panels are compared to the austere geometry and exposed metal and concrete of Bartle Hall. While the latter building is needed exactly where it is placed, since it serves to augment the now limited spaces of the Municipal Auditorium, the new exhibition hall, visually, would be more at home in an environment made up of structures such as the two stadiums of the Truman Sports Complex, or the Kemper Arena. This last is another important facility that was completed in 1976, just in time to house

164

Fig. 184. BIOLOGICAL SCIENCES (left) and the SPENCER CHEMISTRY BUILDINGS, Volker Campus, University of Missouri-Kansas City. Completed in 1972, Kivett & Myers architects. (photo 1977)

the Republican National Convention that year.

The R. Crosby Kemper Memorial Arena (Fig. 183) is located in the West Bottoms on land that was cleared when the stockyards operation was greatly reduced after the closure of most of the packing houses. Designed by C. F. Murphy & Associates of Chicago, Kemper Arena is an AIA Honor Award winner as an outstanding example of new architecture. Of special note are the external structural trusses that provide for a 324-foot roof-span over the multi-purpose arena that can seat 16-18,000 people. It is worth noting the obvious, that the Kemper Arena, the Bartle Exhibition Hall, and the twin stadiums share a similarity in that the structural system provides the principal stylistic features. The result is that each structure is a bold shape without ornament, where cast shadows form much of the surface interest. Textures are those of the structural materials, and very little of the structural system is concealed—ex-

cept perhaps behind a coat of paint. In many ways the same is true of the Crown Center complex, though there, considerable amounts of veneer or cladding are used. Still, the emphasis is on large simple shapes, but now with constructivist organization. A great deal of the surface is concrete, straight from the forms, or in precast panels.

This interest in large shapes, somewhat constructivist in arrangement, can be found in a building whose construction on the University of Missouri-Kansas City campus was also interrupted by the long construction strikes. Its exterior exposes large areas of concrete, though stone cladding is also used. This is the Kenneth A. Spencer Chemistry Building, which was designed and built concurrently with the adjacent Biological Sciences Building (Fig. 184). The architects were Kivett & Myers, and the buildings were completed in 1972. The projecting shapes on the facades of the chemistry building contain the ductwork for fume hoods and the like, and we can see some variations from bay to bay. This departure from a rigorous repetition of design elements can be seen also in the windows, which vary in size and frequency, from bay to bay, giving this building a far more interesting appearance than otherwise would have been the case. The sharply defined forms on the exterior are given some surface treatment through the linear subdivisions of the stone cladding, which define floor levels, and the recessed lines on the concrete which repeat the profile of the staircase in the end unit.

The bold geometry of this UMKC building contrasts strongly with the older architecture on the campus (e.g. Figs. 120 and 133), but it does relate very nicely to the nearby Library Building (Fig. 167) without duplicating its appearance. The library anticipates the more dramatically arranged forms of the chemistry building, but the elegance in proportions, the disciplined regularity, and the complete concealment of concrete behind two kinds of stone, make the design of the library more a product of the sixties than is the case of the chemistry building though it was designed at the end of that decade.

The library's architects, Marshall & Brown, were responsi-

Fig. 186. SOUTHWESTERN BELL TELEPHONE COMPANY BUILDING, 500 E. Eighth. Completed in 1973, Kivett & Myers architects. (photo 1977)

Fig. 185. PENN VALLEY COLLEGE (partial view from the north), 3201 Southwest Trafficway. Opened in 1973, Marshall & Brown architects. (photo 1978)

ble for the building-complex that forms Penn Valley Community College. The College, at 31st and Southwest Trafficway (Fig. 185), was opened for use in 1973. Here the wall expanses of sheer brick are relieved only by clean-cut openings and the constructivist composition of the several building components. Many other buildings of the 1970s are similar in style, some in brick, and some using precast cladding as in the case of the new Southwestern Bell Telephone Company (Fig. 186) at 500 East Eighth. This is a Kivett & Myers design, also of 1973.

Perhaps the most noticeable change in style in the seventies, from that of the sixties, is the definite reduction in the

166

Fig. 188. FARM AND HOME SAVINGS BUILDING, southwest corner 85th and Ward Parkway. Completed in 1974, Richard P. Stahl (Springfield, Mo.) architect. View from the northeast. (photo 1978)

Fig. 189. FARM AND HOME SAVINGS BUILDING, view from the southwest. (photo 1978)

Fig. 187. AMERICAN BANK AND TRUST COMPANY BUILDING, 1 W. Armour. Completed in 1973, Franklin-Frieze & Associates, with Linscott-Haylett consulting, architects. (photo 1978)

Fig. 190. LAKESIDE PLAZA II, 6700 Corporate Drive, Executive Park. Completed in 1977 (design from 1975), Ware and Malcomb (Newport Beach, Cal.) architects. (photo 1978)

amount of glass that is used on the exteriors, while at the same time there is a correspondingly greater stress placed on massive walls, giving a solidity to exteriors that is very different from the homage to the curtain wall that we find in the previous decade (e.g. Fig. 140). However, when glass is used extensively, as in the case of the American Bank Building (Fig. 187), also of 1973, the structural members are given a very important design function. In the American Bank, structure has been externalized, and the curtain wall of glass is two-tiered, reducing the importance that a single plane would have in forming the building's envelope. The bank is a design by Franklin-Frieze & Associates, with Linscott-Haylett Associates consulting, and it is located at the southwest corner of Armour and Main.

One could add to the list of structures built in the 1970s, but mention of four others will suffice to round out major aspects of new developments. One such, noticeable in the seventies, is the departure from rectilinear shapes, used singly as an accent, or in combinations affecting the basic configuration of the building. We begin to find cylindrical forms, walls meeting at other than right angles, and free-form elements and other individualized characteristics appear. These provide striking contrasts to the shapes of the sixties. An example of this can be found in the Farm and Home Savings Office which opened late in 1974 at the southwest corner of 85th and Ward Parkway (Figs. 188 and 189). The architect was Richard P. Stahl of Springfield, Missouri. We have also noted the growing use of concrete, both site-poured and precast, and of brick in providing exteriors with massive shapes and substantial textural surfaces. On smaller structures, wood panelling on the exterior has become more common, and it is often used to provide a similar, overall effect.

At Executive Park, an evolving development at Interstate 435 and Front Street, there are two office structures identified as Lakeside Plaza I and II. The second one (Fig. 190), though completed in 1977, is a duplicate of the first which was designed in 1975 by Ware & Malcomb of Newport Beach, California. Here the entire structural system is placed outside of the glass envelope, and it is clad in red cedar. Given the

Fig. 191. CITY CENTER SQUARE, Eleventh to Twelfth, Main to Baltimore. Completed in 1977, Skidmore, Owings & Merrill architects. View from the southeast. (photo 1978)

167

shape and placement of the supporting columns, and the door enframement and other features, the result is a rather sculptural structure that at a distance seems to hover above the flatness of the bottom land on which it is located.

Then there is City Center Square (Fig. 191), a Skidmore, Owings & Merrill design that was nearly complete by the end of 1976, opening in spring of the following year. This thirty-story building, using a reinforced concrete structure,

168

Fig. 192. Atrium in retail section of CITY CENTER SQUARE. (photo 1978)

lower level of the building is pierced by a four-story diagonal lobby that is roofed by a glazed, prismatic framework and it is crossed by several pedestrian bridges (Fig. 192). On the exterior, there is a somewhat formidable sense of weight and bulk that is reinforced by the slot-like window openings, which though quite large, are not large enough, proportionally, to reduce the dominance of the precast-clad grid. It is especially interesting to compare this design with that of the earlier SOM design, the BMA Building (Fig. 156), where the exterior grid is decidedly less domineering. The difference is an index to the shift in design values over a decade's time.

Not quite as heavy in appearance, but still an example of the more massive look of the seventies, is the office tower completed in 1974 which was designed by Harry Weese of Chicago for the Mercantile Bank and Trust Company (with Patty, Berkebile & Nelson associated, Fig. 192). Located at the southeast corner of Walnut and Eleventh, due west of the Bryant Building (Fig. 109), it is rather different in appearance than its neighbor. Where the Bryant stands solidly rooted to the ground, with a vertical flow that steps back at the top, the Mercantile Bank Tower is poised above a corner plaza, perched on steel columns. Behind the plaza, which is partly sunken, there is a subservient block; and the tower appears to rest lightly on a stilted platform. Also in contrast to the Bryant, there is a strong horizontal feeling to the Mercantile's grid of metal and tinted glass, due in part to the recessed spandrels. While it makes for an odd neighbor to the Bryant Building, it is an appropriate companion to the City Center Square that is nearby.

While such large structures were typically designed in the most recent of contemporary styles, smaller structures often exhibited a curious return to historic eclecticism. In some instances there was a good reason to use some historic style or prototype in a new building, especially when it was intended to expand an existing complex of an earlier era, but in most cases the choices are open to question. Examples of this need not be illustrated, since the use of historic styles in recent

grows out of a four-level banking, retail and restaurant section, all placed over an underground garage for 400 cars. Occupying at ground level a full city block, from Eleventh to Twelfth, from Main to Baltimore, the total structure encompasses some 650,000 square feet of rentable space. The visual weight of the tower, which is at the northwest corner of the block, is reduced by the use of an uneven hexagonal plan that is given emphasis by extensions at the lower levels that stage outward and downward to the full extent of the lot. The

Fig. 193. MERCANTILE BANK TOWER, 1101 Walnut. Completed in 1974, Harry Weese & Associates (Chicago) architects. (photo 1978)

years has become rather superficial and even badly done when compared to the 1910s or 20s. The significance of 1970s' historicism lies in the evidence it furnishes that there is a reaction to the stylistic uniformities of the previous two decades. While some architects seem to have been propelled into investigations of the constructivist or brutalist approach to design, to avoid producing simple rectilinear solids of the sort that had occurred so frequently, others turned to selecting features from historic styles.

Historic eclecticism had not died out in the fifties and sixties, but it had become sufficiently attenuated to seem nothing more than a lingering, outmoded trend. However, starting in the middle-sixties, a renewal of interest can be detected, manifested first in the design of tract houses and garden apartment buildings, and later in other structures. Truly eclectic in approach, one finds strange combinations, and once again mansard roofs have become popular. There are Georgian porticos, medieval arches, and simulated half-timbering which appear in various ways on buildings not particularly related to the style of the ornamental features. On occasion, one finds a more systematic use of the Georgian or the Tudor style, but without the fine detailing common in the period right before and after World War I.

This interest in the older styles, even if superficially executed, was apparently motivated in part by a reaction to the more minimalist styles of contemporary modernism. It also appears to be motivated by a growing nostalgia on the part of clients for a world that is rapidly vanishing, vanishing as it recedes in time but also as demolitions remove tangible evidence of the past. The earlier years, whatever their inadequacies, seem attractive to many when compared to the tensions and traumas of the more impersonalized present. This type of nostalgia, however, is not the motivation for another form of interest in older structures. Here we speak of the serious and professionally-supported interest in what we call historic preservation. This is a movement which does not support historic eclecticism as a modern style of architecture.

As we noted earlier, historic preservationists responded to various stimuli at the turn of the decade, and in the 1970s, forces were joined to make this an important movement in

the city. Despite some failures, its strength has grown to where it has an increasingly important influence on the architectural history of the city. In Kansas City, preservationism has operated under several distinct sponsorships. There is, of course, the Landmarks Commission which was created in 1970 and reorganized under a stronger ordinance in 1977. In 1974, the Historic Kansas City Foundation was organized. It assumed various tasks, but a critically important portion of its mission is the purchase of endangered structures and their resale with restrictions that limit inappropriate changes or later demolition. The Foundation has had some important successes and is becoming more effective each year. As noted, the Jackson County Historical Society has been involved in architectural preservation for a number of years.

Central to the preservation movement is the objective of halting unwarranted demolition or radical remodeling of historically or architecturally significant buildings. If we look at such buildings, and the problems involved in their preservation, we can see that there are two different approaches which can be used to meet the challenges of conserving our built heritage. The most common approach, and in many ways the one with the best record of success, is that of concentrating on individual buildings whose significance is readily demonstrated, and the preservation case can be argued and supported on the merits of the specific structure.

The other and more difficult approach, hence with fewer achievements, is the attempt to preserve buildings in groups, within historic districts. Ranging from a few adjacent buildings to an entire neighborhood, district-preservation is for many, despite the inherent difficulties, the only meaningful way to ensure that the preservation movement will have a vital role in maintaining the historical integrity of a city. Each situation, however, whether individual or district, presents its own peculiarities. In Kansas City the difficulties in coping with these peculiarities has demonstrated the advantages of operating through on-going organizations rather than on an emergency, ad hoc basis. The loss of the Burnham & Root Board of Trade Building in 1968 was a case of too few people and no organization trying to cope with a commercial building that had been neglected for decades, and it was too late to effect much leverage.

The Union Station crisis beginning in 1971 was an even more overwhelming problem, but here the importance of the building, given its size, its place in the urban landscape, and in people's memories, made it something of a popular rallying point—something that could not be done for the Board of Trade. A large number of individuals became involved on an ad hoc basis, but this stimulated organized action. Demolition was forestalled, and while it is hard to say exactly how much of an influence preservationists had in this, it is this writer's considered opinion that they played an important role in halting precipitous action. The point of importance, however, is that in contrast with the Board of Trade case, this time a Landmarks Commission existed and became involved, officially representing the public's interest in the matter. Also, the Union Station crisis captured people's attention, and in the process of dealing with the complex issues associated with the station—for an alternative use had to be found for that giant building—skills were sharpened, and the methodology of coping with crises was tested. Large as the station is, it is still a single-structure problem. Thus the issues of preservation were easily comprehended, and one could readily focus on the building in marshalling support for its preservation. An excellent case study of exactly how this works is the successful rescue effort that saved the Folly Theatre when it was suddenly threatened with demolition.

The Folly (Fig. 194) at Twelfth and Central, was built in 1900, a design of Gunn & Curtiss. In 1973, when the now somewhat bedraggled burlesque house was closed, some key people were aware that the building was a likely candidate for a quick demolition. If this occurred, the last legitimate stage theatre remaining from a great era of the performing arts, designed by major Kansas City architects, would be lost. Appropriate actions were generated by a combination of forces, including the Mayor, members of the Art Commission and the Landmarks Commission, and other concerned people. The goal was to save the structurally sound if shabby building, and to rehabilitate it and make it a significant asset

171

Fig. 194. FOLLY THEATRE, 300 W. Twelfth. Built in 1900 as the Standard Theatre, Gunn & Curtiss architects. Under restoration and renovation by the Performing Arts Foundation, Patty, Berkebile, Nelson & Associates architects. (photo 1978)

for the downtown area. It did not take long to document the building and to have it placed on the National Register. Soon thereafter, the local Performing Arts Foundation, moving purposefully, acquired the structure. They were approved to rehabilitate the building under Missouri Urban Development Law. Though things moved swiftly, this brief account hardly covers all of the steps, stages, and intermediate problems that occurred before one could say, as we can today, that this accoustically bright theatre has been saved, cleaned within, made secure from both the weather and the pigeons, and restoration started.

When the project is completed, the city will have a very fine performing arts auditorium of about 1,000 seats, and though the rehabilitated theatre will not accommodate scenery or staging for a complex show, it will provide a fine resource for most of the performing arts and for lectures and meetings. Located immediately north of the Bartle Exhibition Hall, the Folly augments the city's facilities for conventions and for entertainment. If it had been demolished, the city would not only have lost the only structure of its size and character remaining in the downtown area, but it is unlikely that a downtown replacement would have been built, certainly not at the price required for the Folly's restoration. Thus a 1900 building has been resurrected to appear in the mid-1970s, and because it is a preservation project, it is in many ways a product of the present. Though obviously a building in its eighth decade, it has become an integral part of the recent history of the city, due to the enormous amount of volunteer time and financial contributions that have been given to the project.

Though the Folly is located within a district where hotels and convention facilities are prominent, and arguments for the Folly's preservation stressed this point, it is nevertheless a case of single-structure historic preservation. Elsewhere, there are architectural groupings that argue for district preservation, and these present quite different problems that are part of the city's history in the 1970s.

In residential districts, the task of the preservationists requires tools such as rezoning, reducing red-lining, if not eliminating it altogether, curbing unnecessary demolition, and setting up demonstration projects. In commercial or mixed districts, the identification of viable, new uses for buildings is also needed, and this provides both challenges and frustrations. Two local cases are worth our study if only to point out the fragile foundation on which all of this effort can find itself, and to emphasize the enormity of the problems facing large areas in the older city, especially downtown.

In 1972, largely as the result of one person's vision and effort, an attempt was launched to create new uses for buildings in the heart of Old Town, near the City Market. Named the River Quay, though separated from the river by railroad tracks and flood control dikes, it centered on the three blocks of Delaware between Third and Sixth (Fig. 195), with parts of Walnut, Fifth and Wyandotte Streets also involved. It is here on Delaware that some of the oldest commercial buildings in the city are to be found (Figs. 20, 21 and 33). The buildings became the locations for restaurants, shops, artist studios, and the like, and piecemeal improvement efforts began upgrading the area. In short order, large crowds were attracted and it seemed as if a major achievement in both preservation and renovation was on the way to success. Subsequent events, however, are not so easily described. The original developer sold his interests to outside ownership, whose resources were said to be sufficient to carry out a genuinely fine plan for preservation and revitalization of the area, and there were great expectations. However, other than some early architectural planning and an initial promotional flurry, nothing positive was done, and a decline quickly set in.

Part of the difficulties lay in the fact that there was not then a clearly defined historic district. The developer did not control enough contiguous property to form a secure district for the type of development outlined. Though some key buildings were held, it was difficult to implement a comprehensive plan, and the city had no mechanism to protect the admittedly historic district from encroachments. Further, the financial picture became muddier rather than clearer. There was no significant influx of development money as had been anticipated, and indeed had been pledged. Delay followed delay. Building preservation efforts, though announced, did not take place. Many of the early shop-keepers and artists found little sympathy directed toward them or their investments, or their early efforts to make the River Quay a genuine attraction. Rents were increased. So-called marginal operations, which, in fact, had brought life to the area, were discouraged. This development vacuum, however, was being filled in a way that few at first recognized. Soon it was too late to do anything, if indeed anything could have been done.

172

Fig. 195. RIVER QUAY, Delaware Street looking south from Third, toward the Central Business District. (photo 1974)

174

Fig. 196. WESTPORT SQUARE, at Westport and Pennsylvania. Basic environmental design, Bob Moore architect. Individual interiors by various architects. (photo 1974)

From the first, the River Quay had aimed to be attractive to the general public, to family groups, and so the area was filled with small shops, art galleries, modest-priced restaurants. In addition to the historical values and the window shopping ambience, there was also entertainment offered in the River Quay. With the right ingredients and mix, the River Quay could be a people-magnet from mid-morning to late at night. This indeed was beginning to happen as tourists and locals alike began to visit the Quay. This is what had attracted the outside developer, but it had also attracted another kind of development. Along Wyandotte, but also on Delware, local interests began to open bars that catered to a somewhat different clientele than that envisioned for the River Quay by its early promoters. Efforts were being made to "open up" the River Quay, to serve different values and bawdier tastes. Buildings were outfitted with gaudy signs, and some tacky remodeling began to produce a new image for the otherwise historic area. True, the area had been a red light district at the turn of the century and even later, but that type of historicism was hardly the basis on which to argue the preservation of the structures on Delaware Street. As the district became more tawdry, small shops and artists' studios and almost all of the restaurants closed. By 1976, large sections of the River Quay area had become a garish, nightlife strip, and the development plan once so bravely announced had collapsed.

The new clientele of the River Quay was seeking different pleasures. These were available, but in the competition for business, the district was filled by more bars than were needed, and there simply were not enough customers to go around. This became abundantly clear when the nightlife strip failed to attract the numbers of conventioneers that many bars had anticipated. Competition among these establishments took an ugly turn, and it finally culminated in a series of fires, bombings and murders. The evidence points to underworld involvement in the development and operation of the strip, and this underworld, it was alleged, was troubled by an internal struggle for control. This in turn affected the area, and by 1977 the River Quay idea was dead, dead even for the underworld's enterprises. Assaults on people and buildings, leading to the total destruction of several structures, had driven away even the most hardened customers for the type of nightlife offered on the strip.

The lesson for Kansas City was and is still painfully clear. Preservation of the Old Town district, once called the River Quay, required a combination of: a control of all relevant properties by a single responsible organization; the support of government units; and a viable architectural and economic plan. It is hard to say whether or not the old architecture of Old Town is salvageable in the same sense as the Folly Theatre has proven to be. Some key buildings still stand, some lessons have been learned, and thus there is still some hope.

The lessons of the River Quay were not lost on the developers of Westport Square, in the heart of old Westport (Fig. 196). There, also starting in 1972, basically one square block of what had once been old Westport's downtown was recycled into a district that consists largely of restaurants and specialty shops. Under tight control from the very first by its developers, the exterior of the buildings of Westport Square were left virtually untouched except for some upgrading of condition. The interiors, however, were totally gutted and redesigned to serve diverse contemporary functions. A dismal alley space was converted into an attractive, multi-purpose courtyard (Fig. 197). Located on the south side of Westport Road, between Broadway and Pennsylvania, Westport Square is across from the Boone Trading Post (Fig. 4) and the site of the Harris House Hotel (Fig. 5). The buildings that form the Square, however, are not in themselves either historically or architecturally significant. But there is a homogeneity in the many small buildings from an earlier era. With imaginatively done interiors, attractive shops and restaurants, and the courtyard, Westport Square has succeeded where River Quay failed. In fact, it has succeeded so well it has generated concerns that the surrounding area may be overdeveloped, with less rigorous controls of course, and this would be to the detriment of all. As these words are being written, Westport Square seems sound and safe under vigilant care, but its success will always lure those who could kill it as certainly as the River Quay was killed.

The violent death of the River Quay is a grim image and it

175

176

Fig. 197. Portion of the courtyard in WESTPORT SQUARE, a recycling project that weds the old and the new. (photo 1978)

is heeded by those who have a stake, cultural or economic, in effective preservation through recycled use of commercial buildings. Unfortunately, the lessons learned do not provide the means to solve the many problems associated with affecting a successful marriage between new developments and historic preservation. But there are a growing number of accomplishments that provide positive lessons to augment those learned from the River Quay, and these are being put to good use. An important agency in this educational program, as well as being an activist organization, is the Historic Kansas City Foundation. Even while it was in its formative year (1974), it was pressed into action to save a threatened building. Though hardly ready to meet its own organizational needs, it assumed major responsibilities and proved to be indeed a capable force in the preservation of the city's architecture. Privately constituted, it works closely with the Landmarks Commission. Much has been accomplished, but much yet remains to be done.

So as the city concluded one hundred and fifty years of development, we draw our history to a close in the year the nation celebrated its Bicentennial. In that year a much needed Tax Reform Act was enacted, and it introduced new incentives to preserve and rehabilitate historic structures. As we survey the scene, we can see both new construction and examples of effective preservation. We also see that the old and the new in architecture can, with adequate advance planning, work together for the general good of the city. That is a comforting thought to hold as we await the next episodes in the architectural history of Kansas City, Missouri.

177

178

Detail from Fig. 63

Bibliography

The primary library collection that one can consult for a study of Kansas City's architectural history is that of the Missouri Valley Room of the Kansas City, Missouri Public Library. Also in that library, newspapers and old City Directories are readily available on microfilm. The Missouri Valley Room's holdings are diverse and not easily described. They range from photographs, maps and newspaper cuttings, through regular and ephemeral publications of all types, to the Archives of the Native Sons of Kansas City. As in any special collections situation, the guidance and assistance of the librarians and archivists is the key to effective access to the collections and to their use. The staff of the Missouri Valley Room is remarkably patient and genuinely interested in helping people although under constant and widely disparate demands upon their limited time.

At the University of Missouri-Kansas City Library, the Special Collections contain a smaller but still very useful body of published material, and in addition there are some useful graduate theses. A major resource at UMKC, which as of this writing is still being prepared for public use, is the Architectural Records Collections that consists of several thousand rolls of blueprints, some drawings and related materials associated with Kansas City architecture. Access to the Special Collections materials is initiated with the librarians in the General Reference Room.

The Landmarks Commission has a growing archive of material derived from a variety of sources, many not readily accessible to the general public, and the Historic Kansas City Foundation has a developing archive and library. However, these two collections have been formed to further the work of the organizations and to assist professional investigators, and thus they are not designed or arranged for use by the general public. Finally, the Kansas City Museum has some valuable materials in its library, as does the Research Library and Archives of the Jackson County Historical Society.

The published materials used for the preparation of this history fall into three categories. First, there are those publications that are basic to a study of the city's general history. This is a fairly short list and, as one might expect, there is a degree of repetition in their contents. Some errors of fact do occur, and some are repeated; however, some cross-checking of sources is usually sufficient to correct these. Second, there are the comparatively few publications that deal with the architectural history of the city. Third, there are the serial publications that contain, with some frequency, data relevant to a study of this sort. The references cited below are not intended to be an exhaustive listing, but they should be sufficient to orient a reader to the materials used in the preparation of this history.

General Publications

Spaulding, Charles C. *Annals of the City of Kansas.* Kansas City: Van Horn & Abeel, 1858. Reprinted by Frank Glenn Publishing Co., 1950.

Miller, William H. *Early History of Kansas City.* Kansas City: Birdsall & Miller, 1881.

Case, Theodore S. (ed.). *History of Kansas City, Missouri*. Syracuse: D. Mason & Co., 1888.

Whitney, Carrie Westlake. *Kansas City, Missouri, Its History and Its People*. 3 vols. Chicago: S. J. Clarke Publishing Co., 1908.

Ellis, Roy. *A Civic History of Kansas City, Missouri*. Springfield: Elkins-Sawyer, 1930.

Where These Rocky Bluffs Meet. Kansas City: The Chamber of Commerce, 1938.

Haskell, Henry C. Jr., and Fowler, Richard B. *City of the Future*. Kansas City: Frank Glenn Publishing Co., 1950.

Glaab, Charles N. *Kansas City and the Railroads*. Madison: The State Historical Society of Wisconsin, 1962.

Brown, A. Theodore. *Frontier Community, Kansas City to 1870*. Columbia: University of Missouri Press, 1963.

Dorsett, Lyle W. *The Pendergast Machine*. New York: Oxford University Press, 1968.

Brown, A. Theodore, and Dorsett, Lyle W. *K. C., A History of Kansas City, Missouri*. Boulder: Pruett Publishing Company, 1978. (Published after the completion of our manuscript on the city's architectural history.)

Architectural Publications

When it comes to publications dealing with the architectural history of the city, our sources are severely limited. There are a number of periodical articles scattered through the years and the journals, but other than Frank Maynard Howe, "The Development of Architecture in Kansas City, Missouri," *Architectural Record* XV, 2 (Feb., 1904), 134-157, none is what one would call a "must read" piece. The Howe article qualifies because the author was of Van Brunt & Howe, and Howe, Hoit & Cutler; and the date is within a period of change in Kansas City's history. In addition, there are four books which merit special attention.

Bryan, John Albury. *Missouri's Contribution to American Architecture*. St. Louis: St. Louis Architectural Club, 1928.

This includes both illustrations and text which are valuable, though proportionately very little of the book deals with Kansas City.

Mitchell, Giles Carroll. *There is no Limit: Architecture and Sculpture in Kansas City*. Kansas City: Brown-White Co., 1934.

This is a basic source book, but not a particularly scholarly one. It is the work of an architect who knew and had an opportunity to talk to key personnel. The book is a series of entries on individual structures or sculptures.

Wilson, William H. *The City Beautiful Movement in Kansas City*. Columbia: University of Missouri Press, 1964.

This provides a valuable insight into George Kessler's work on the parks and boulevards, and how it affected architectural developments.

Kansas City, A Place in Time. Kansas City: Landmarks Commission, 1977.

This is a useful listing with illustrations and brief commentaries of a representative group of extant structures, erected prior to 1950, deserving of attention.

Pending, as of this writing, is a guidebook to the city's architecture which is being prepared by the Kansas City Chapter of the American Institute of Architects, with publication expected in mid-1979.

In addition, there are a number of view-books, mostly published in the early years of this century, which provide a wealth of visual information but with very little documentation. These are very useful for the student of the city's architecture who is interested in the city's appearance as of the early twentieth century.

Serials

In addition to the newspaper files, there are a very small handful of local publications that contain useful information. The Kansas City Chapter of the American Institute of Architects once published a journal, *Skylines*, later the *Midwest Architect*; these journals merit perusal by the serious investigator. The *Western Contractor*, now the *Midwest Contractor*, likewise has proven useful. Currently, the bi-monthly *Historic Kansas City News*, published by the Historic Kansas City Foundation, is the only serial that regularly carries items dealing specifically with Kansas City's architectural history.

180

Index

184

Index

185

KANSAS CITY, MISSOURI
AN ARCHITECTURAL HISTORY
1826-1976

was designed by David E. Spaw,
photocomposed in Intertype Trump Mediaeval,
and printed on Warren's Flokote Enamel
by
The Lowell Press, Kansas City, Missouri